this book is dedicated
to everyone who helped

a garden
& three houses

words jane brown
pictures richard bryant captions
Margaret and Peter Aldington

The authors are indebted to Whitby, Bird and Partners for their sponsorship

ISBN 1 870673 32 8

British Library Cataloguing-in-Publication Data
A catalogue record for this book is available from the British Library.

Published in Great Britain by Garden Art Press, a division of Antique Collectors' Club Ltd
Book layout – Peter Aldington from a design by Michael Thierens. Production – Michael Taylor
Drawings on pages 32, 38, 46, 52, 66 & 71 by Ronald Wilson
The drawing on page 36 by John Hookham is reproduced by permission of Cambridge University Press
Colour origination by Graphic Ideas Studios
Set in Frutiger Light, printed in England by Antique Collectors' Club Ltd., Woodbridge, Suffolk.

contents

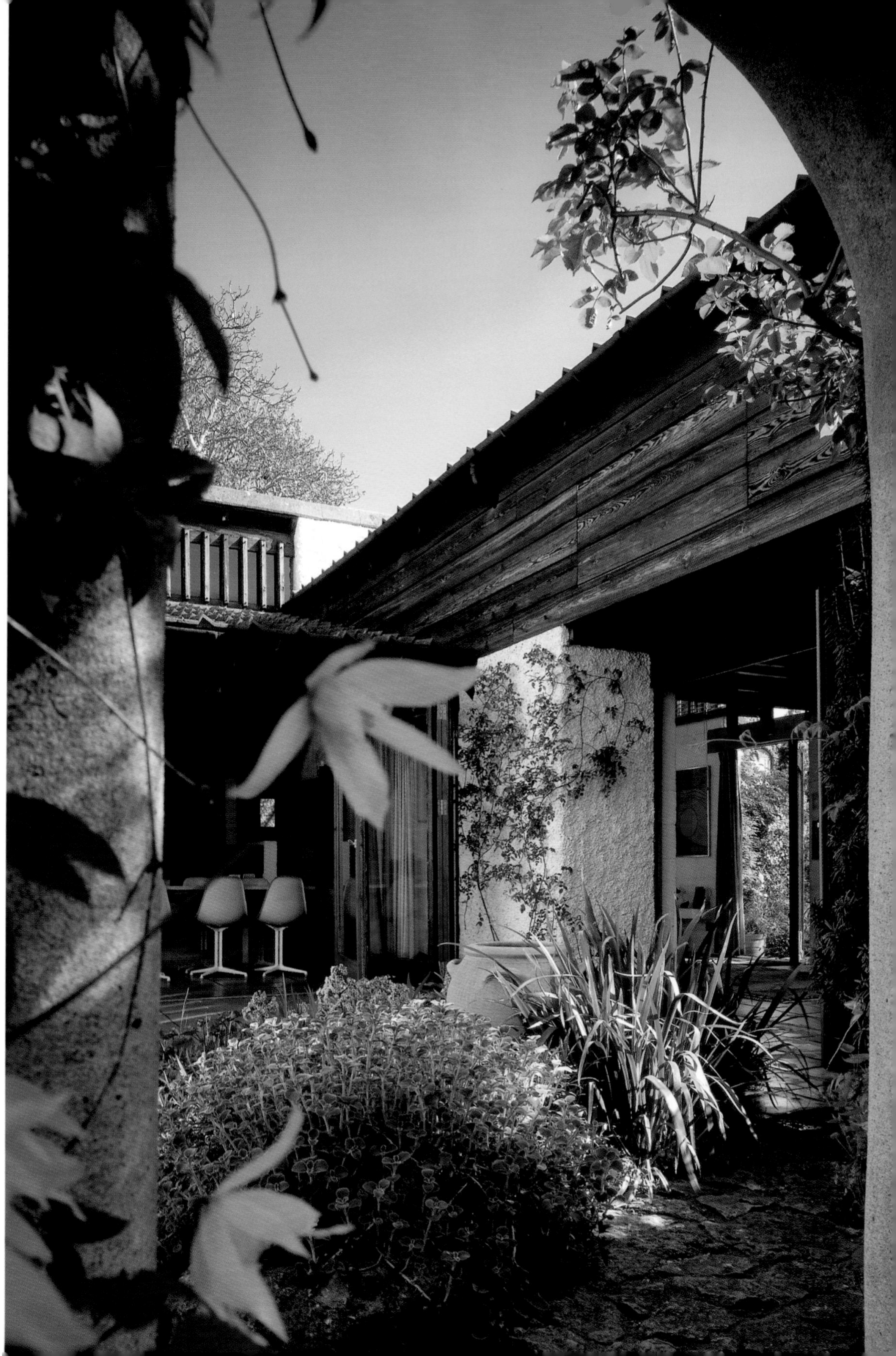

foreword

Thirty years ago Peter Aldington added three houses to the village of Haddenham in Buckinghamshire. Today these houses and their gardens stand mature as a rare example of how to add modern houses to an ancient village without a hint of suburbia.

The villages of England are a precious heritage of architecture and landscape renowned world wide as habitable places. It is no wonder that people flock to live in them. Most villages near large towns, and almost all in South-East England, are targets for new houses and most have suffered from poor planning and bad design. Trees are lost, roads widened; the bye-laws which failed to improve suburbs are applied to wreck the traditions of rural building. The Aldingtons had to fight road widening, the building line and the felling of trees. But they won and achieved a modern statement of the village tradition, with compactness and privacy, variety and unity. And of course they preserved several fine trees, one or two of which are intimately close to the larger house, which is the architect's own.

The group is memorable also for the architect's garden; a superb composition of widely differing spaces of which one is always aware from the house. The garden cradles and enfolds the house. It is really several gardens which take advantage of the irregular boundary to create many spaces of various sizes, some incorporating old walls and outer buildings, each with its own scale and character. The house and its garden cover little more than half an acre. I know of no other garden which packs such riches into so small a space with such beautiful and interesting plants.

Peter Shepheard

pages 8 and 9
left:
A stone path leads through an old wall into the courtyard of our house, Turn End. *Asphodeline lutea* in the foreground.
Right:
Autumn and the long vista in Turn End's garden.

These pages:
The old and the new:
Opposite:
A large stoneware urn with naturalised planting and a century old ivy clad apple tree which now plays host to rose 'Cérise Bouquet'
Left:
An acacia tree (*Robinia pseudoacacia*) now embraced by house and pool

Light and shade, night and day:
Opposite:
Turn End dining room and
Left:
A corner of the living room where a glazed roof links an old wall to the new house.

introduction

This is the story of three houses, designed and built as a village housing scheme at Haddenham in Buckinghamshire in the 1960s. They have since become internationally celebrated, even elevated to the status of listed buildings as 'exceptional and influential' examples of modern architecture.[1] The scheme was designed by a young architect, Peter Aldington, and built, to a great extent with their own hands, by him and his wife, Margaret. One of the houses, Turn End, has been the Aldingtons' family home ever since, and Turn End and its glorious garden are the major stars of this book; the other two houses, The Turn and Middle Turn, are equally important but as private homes with smaller gardens, they have rather quieter lives.

The accompanying photographs will have already revealed the qualities of these unassuming landmarks of modern design which, far from shouting their presence, are tucked away discreetly down a winding village street in middle England. People who have known the houses for years, who may even have helped to build them, are unanimously lyrical on their beauty and the joy of returning visits; old friends and new visitors seem equally converted by them to the virtues of modern architecture. Perhaps all these expressions of pleasure are tinged with an underlying surprise that this should be so, but then anyone who has listened to even part of the debate over British architecture of the last forty years will understand. The historian and critic, Dan Cruickshank, visited Turn End in October 1996 for a "Masterclass" article for the journal of the Royal Institute of British Architects: his verdict was that *'these buildings remain an object lesson for all architects'*, and their combination of *'the most modest of materials'*, picturesque traditions, the *'key tenets of modernism'* and a *'magical union'* of indoors and outdoors, made them extraordinary, precious and rare.[2]

It seems almost impossible to celebrate this garden and three houses without a word of

Opposite:
Turn End from the spring garden

Notes:
1. Department of National Heritage, (draft) schedule 1997. Listed Grade 2 July 1998
2. RIBA Journal, October 1996, vol 103, no. 10, pages 56–62.

regret for their rarity value. The twentieth century opened with optimism, with a galaxy of talented architects with Arts and Crafts allegiances, who saw themselves as designers of a domestic continuum – the house, its fixtures and fittings, even fabrics and furniture, and the garden. That the best brains should work on family houses was a radical venture after long centuries of aristocratic dominance: the transformation of Elizabethan and Queen Anne traditions into three-bedroomed semi-detached houses with timbered gables, and into sturdy brick villas, was a brilliant and popular triumph, only marred in that perhaps they outstayed their welcome as design inspirations. By the late twenties it was feared that the gabled and porched British castles set in their garden plots, rippling along avenues, across fields and woods, rather like endless games of patience laid upon the land, were repressively old-fashioned as well as gobbling up too much countryside. Modernism was the perceived solution: new homes of structural steel and wood and concrete, layered and clustered to save space for outdoor activities, with open, flexible interiors full of sunlight and fresh air from big windows, balconies or terraces. Suitable "architectural" plants, aloe, fatsia, monstera, ivies, would share living spaces and terraces, and the rest of the garden was for outdoor leisure and pleasure, according to will, with a preference for a miniature landscape of man-made "wild". Britain was so enthusiastic about modernist ideas in the 1930s, that, amazing as it may seem, the American art historian Henry-Russell Hitchcock was able to write, in 1937, *'it is not altogether an exaggeration to say that England leads the world in modern architectural activity'*.[3]

It was a lead that was lost in the Second World War: against such a major catastrophe it may seem inappropriate to call it a loss at all, but the consequent shortcomings for British housing, even architecture in general, have not been insignificant. After the war, modern architecture needed to be revived and re-defined in the midst of rebuilding. The architect, Lionel Esher, was part of that rebuilding and has been its historian as well:[4] Lord Esher also appears in the following pages, in the story of Turn End, and he has recently written *'It is good to be reminded that it is still just about the best postwar house I know'*.[5]

Notes:
3. Henry-Russell Hitchcock, Modern Architecture in England, New York 1937 quoted in A Different World: Emigré Architects in Britain 1928–38, Charlotte Benton, 1995, p 73.
4. Lionel Esher, various writings but particularly A Broken Wave, The Rebuilding of Britain, 1940–1980, 1981.
5. Letter to Peter Aldington, dated 31 Dec 1990.

When we bought the site in Haddenham, partly an old orchard, it was carpeted with snowdrops… and still is.

A corner of the studio at Turn End. A wichert wall (pitted by wild bees), part of the original gardener's shed, provides a richly textured backdrop and lives happily with the materials of the modern building.

the people

One of Peter Aldington's few maxims is that *'to make a building well assumes an understanding of people – to build otherwise is degrading'*. His first thoughts on a village housing project were that it should combine past traditions and modern technology to create homes as refuges from the hurly-burly of everyday living. The site in Haddenham, bought in early 1963, was to be the test-bed for his planned process of listening to the past, making a building of the present that would serve for the future. He and Margaret did not consider that this included their own indefinite futures, but clearly the demonstration would only become valid if they were prepared to live in one of the houses. They were to be "the people" in their own experiment, but this was to prove one of the least demanding of their many roles.

When they married in April 1962, they were both approaching thirty; Margaret was nursing in Glasgow, and Peter was an architect in London. Their passions for mountains and wild places had brought them together, and were to sustain them in their building adventures to come.

Margaret was brought up in the north-east of England, where her father was docks mechanical engineer in Hartlepool. She wanted to be a vet, virtually impossible for a girl in the early 1950s, but discovered her alternative vocation in nursing. After general and psychiatric training at the Middlesex Hospital she regained her Scottish roots by moving to Glasgow. Except for when she was building Turn End, and when Clair, born 1968, and Rachel, born 1970, were small, Margaret has continued nursing, working in health and community projects, and even fitting in seven years as a local councillor. She confesses *'I only came to terms with being a housewife because I built the house'* – a revelation of her characteristic dignity and determination.

Peter was born in Preston, where his father, Dr John Aldington, worked for Siemens and played

The simple lines of this antique table – a retirement present to Peter's father – our Victorian mountain pictures, painting and other objects all transcend their eras to live harmoniously with their modern surroundings in Turn End's living room

a pioneering role in the development of fluorescent and other modern lighting. He went to Preston Grammar School, and in 1951, to Manchester University School of Architecture, completing the diploma course in 1956. He immediately joined the Housing Division of the London County Council Architect's Department, where he was to stay until late 1962, with two years out for compulsory national service.

For Peter, mountaineering had preceded architecture, and rock gardens – imitating mountains – had come before both: his first construction, inspired by the precise and copious details in Symons-Jeune's Natural Rock Gardening[6] was a fairly modest schoolboy effort in the garden at Preston. When Dr Aldington's work took the family south to Keston in Kent, they inherited an ex-Chelsea Flower Show rock garden which Peter restored. Rhododendrons and ericaceous plants won his gardening loyalty.

Rock garden construction and mountaineering are interesting apprenticeships for an architect, and there seems a natural logic in the resulting tactile, sculptural approach to understanding building materials and exploring their uses. Peter Aldington is an architect through and through, to his fingertips, always thinking about the job or jobs in hand, treating the problems and pleasures much the same, teasing out a solution before he goes to the drawing board. He feels himself to be a maker of buildings, he works at 'making connections and creating forms which enclose spaces for people to use and enjoy'. It is an attractive notion, and will obviously work for a garden as well as a house.

It is worth adding that the Aldingtons had no great store of funds when they set out on their idealistic scheme. Peter had a basic allowance from his father, and they had savings and a shrewd and supportive bank manager, a species quite common in the sixties, though now almost extinct. The necessity for the bank's support only

Margaret and Peter Aldington on holiday in 1963

emphasised the speculative nature of their plans, their dependence upon their own skills, hard work and luck. As speculation in any guise was anathema to the architectural profession, Margaret was to be the developer, the owner and client for the Turn End project, and her husband was her architect.

Note:
6. B H B Symons-Jeune, Natural Rock Gardening, Country Life 1932, 2nd ed 1936.

The coach house in Turn End garden now houses garden artifacts and a band saw once used by Walter Rose.
(see page 35)

retrospect

It seems apt that it was in 1951, the year of the Festival of Britain, which then seemed the new dawn of modern architecture, that Peter started his diploma course at Manchester University's architecture school. Five years later, in gravitating to the Housing Division of the London County Council's Architect's department, he arrived at the ideological and innovatory heart of the liberal modernist wing of his profession. In November of that year, 1956, the Architectural Review splashed more than twenty pages lauding and illustrating the department's work, especially the schemes at the Alton Estate, Roehampton, and Albert Drive, Wimbledon, where the exciting high-rise blocks of flats teetered elegantly amongst undulating lawns.[7] This was the cutting edge of progressive architecture; this was the place to be. The brave new group initiative system employed hundreds of architects, and rubbing shoulders with one's fellows (there were few women in those days) was never dull, there was a buzz in the professional air, it was provocative and stimulating. It is also worth noting that much was made then of a new commandment, that it was essential to save mature trees wherever possible, for the benefit of new buildings.

In this heady atmosphere Peter Aldington confirmed his architectural heroes. Le Corbusier was well established, and James Stirling was soon added, especially for his tough, yet dignified, low-cost flats on Ham Common, designed with James Gowan… 'a scheme immediately recognised for its power and logic'.[8] In the unmissable Review, James Stirling wrote of his pilgrimage to Le Corbusier's 'crab shell' church at Ronchamp, dubbed poetry in concrete. Stirling wondered in awe at the whitewashed, hand-thrown rendering, 'with an impasto of about two inches', and at the quality of the light filtered in through white tunnels in the thick walls. 'Functionalism', pronounced Stirling in praise, 'remains in Europe the essentially humanist method of designing to a specific use'.[9] For the young London architects, the

Notes:
7. Robert Furneaux Jordan, feature on London County Council, Architectural Review, November 1956.
8. Charles Jencks, Modern Movements in Architecture, 1973, (1980 ed) p 262.
9. James Stirling On Ronchamp, Architectural Review, March 1956, p 155.

'plastic inventiveness' (another Stirling phrase) of functionalism, was confirmed by the "This is Tomorrow" exhibition at the Whitechapel Gallery in 1956. Peter Aldington recalls that he and his friends realised 'and for the first time for a lot of us' how the building materials that they tended to take for granted 'had an inherent æsthetic quality peculiar to themselves in their untrammelled state'.

However, in the late fifties, the virtues of wood, concrete and glass in virgin states had to remain a private passion. The business of architects was the rebuilding of Britain on a magnum scale: everything was getting bigger. New towns, power stations, factories, hospitals and schools filled the pages of the architectural magazines, demonstrating a professional magicianship with "system building" and budgets. With such giants abroad in the land the lowly but precious qualities of human scale were trampled underfoot. Of course, there were exceptions: the Hertfordshire schools, the housing for Loddon Rural District Council in north Norfolk, the SPAN housing, and many other schemes where the architect proved to be a sensitive member of the human race.[10] But, the cry went up, the sense of community in small towns and villages was being annihilated up and down the land by the imposition of bye-law development, which decreed acres of tarmac, wind-torn expanses of grass, and rows of forlorn boxes in fields, in the name of new housing estates. While architectural expertise built palaces for industry, the homes of men and women – arguably the most serious concern for any architect – were subject to a 'heartless laissez faire... that starts with an indifferent design indifferently detailed and then repeats it'. In the Architectural Review Ian Nairn campaigned against this intrinsic neglect for over a decade: he cursed 'the false use of local idiom', the negation of any building pattern or grouping possessed by an old community, and repeatedly identified 'the fearful state of rural housing' as the epitome of bad housing design in general. If rural housing could

be re-vitalised, freed from the bye-law chains, then the whole face of Britain, let alone the people, would benefit.[11]

Such challenging notions were much discussed by young architects as they bent over their drawing boards, and undoubtedly aired in the County Hall canteen. All architects are exhorted to bring their individual solutions to bear on gigantic problems, and to believe that they can make a difference. It was hardly surprising then, that when Peter Aldington went on a winter climbing course in early 1960, and found himself with a commission for 'a modern interpretation of a cottage' from fellow climbers, Mike and Celia White, he grasped it with both hands.

Notes:
10. See Paul Mauger, Buildings in the Country, A Mid-Century Assessment, Batsford 1959.
11. Ian Nairn, particularly the Architectural Review, October 1968, Rural Housing, p 228.

Trees in many guises make statements in both houses and garden. The railway sleeper steps far left are identical in size to the beams over door and window. The frequency of the mullions conveys a tree-like quality to this large opening, thereby giving both privacy and light.

askett green

The "White House" was to be built on a tiny plot, only thirty-five feet deep, on a small green in the centre of the hamlet of Askett, outside Princes Risborough in Buckinghamshire. Perhaps with Ronchamp hovering at the back of his mind, Peter Aldington considered the essentials of a cottage… *'tiny windows, low ceilings and head bumping beams and doorways'*. The beams were oversize, *'large, chunky things in small spaces'* which built up a unique sense of scale. The reconciliation of these essentials with the site, the budget, and the building bye-laws and regulations, was the making of his first building, Askett Green, which Mike and Celia White still happily inhabit. In the architect's words *'it is a strongly modelled box of white painted brick and black stained concrete, which supports and contains a timber secondary structure'*.

For the present-day visitor, this is a box of surprises. The small, timbered hall, fitted with ingenious flaps and slides and an open storage loft, opens out into a double height, "heart of the house" room, with a south wall of glass transforming the light from an enclosed court. Out from this airy, light space are pushed *'the low and compressed spaces'*, the sitting room, which is really a generous alcove, the dining room and kitchen. Before the walls were painted white these spaces were too dark to work in, and the builder had to have the lights on all day, *'but this to me'*, says the architect, *'is what a cottage is all about'*. A more than substantial – "massive" – timber stair rises from the central space to a balcony landing (this is a cottage with its own minstrels' gallery) and the bedrooms, warm but airy cells beneath the roof.

Askett Green is very self-contained; it allows for a few pieces of decorative furniture, but most of its fittings are part of itself. Like a well-disciplined Topsy, it grew: its brick walls *'started extending to support concrete kitchen benches, concrete corbels grew out of the walls to carry*

Opposite:
The philosophy of simple, almost peasant-like timber detailing, and walls which 'grew' into seats, shelves, steps and storage units in Askett Green's interior was developed further at Haddenham.

Top:
Askett Green from the south
Below:
The street facade is pierced
only by the front door.

Opposite, top:
The house, although
unapologetically modern, has
a scale which relates to its
older neighbours and helps to
define the tiny green.
Photos Richard Einzig/Arcaid

joist-sized pieces of timber which became bookshelves or seats'. 'Maybe', the architect muses, *'it is a piece of hollow, functional sculpture which one lives inside?'.* He does not object to the Corbusian catchphrase *'a machine for living'.*

The site, surrounded by other houses, had dictated a blank wall facing the green to prevent Askett Green from becoming a goldfish bowl. 'Monstrosity' was the predictable comment of a local councillor when it was being built; when it was finished, the local paper crooned over it, with headlines *'Spacious, Beautiful and Exciting'.*[12] For human interest there was a photograph of a young couple posing rather self-consciously on the stairs; these were the Aldingtons at home, for as Mike and Celia White had to go abroad, they rented Askett Green to Peter and Margaret as their first home. This was on condition that they

finished it, sanding and varnishing the interior wood, painting the walls and making the garden.

For the architectural papers Askett Green was photographed by Richard Einzig, who was Peter's neighbour in the LCC drawing office, as his first architectural photography commission. They were brilliant photographs and drew attention to the house, especially in the continental papers and in an important piece in Ideal Home magazine.[13]

In the late summer of 1962 Peter left the LCC for the Timber Research and Development Association, where he hoped for opportunities to exploit the architectural properties of wood, but he was soon disappointed. Ever more convinced that he wanted to build on the experience of Askett Green and demonstrate that village housing could be both modern and traditional, he kept his eyes open for a suitable building site.

Above:
The 'suitable building site'

Notes:
12. Bucks Advertiser, January 1963, Turn End scrapbook 1.
13. Richard Einzig soon became the finest architectural photographer of his day: he continued to photograph Aldington+Craig buildings until 1978. In late 1979 he became ill and died in 1980, aged 48

the site

On a snowy morning in early 1963 the Aldingtons were the only bidders at the auction of a building plot in Haddenham, which was withdrawn for failing to reach the reserve. They asked Gosling and Redway of Market Square, Princes Risborough, to negotiate on their behalf, and soon the plot was bought for £3,000, the reserve price.

The half-acre site was between Townside and High Street in Haddenham. It was formerly part of the garden of a big Victorian building on High Street, reputedly the tallest house in Haddenham, once the pride of Freeman Clarke, baker, confectioner, carrier and general entrepreneur of the village. There were wonderful trees, big horse chestnuts, conifers, walnuts, robinias, an evergreen oak, a sequoia and fruit trees in a fragment of former orchard. The vendors, Freeman Clarke's daughters, had placed a covenant on the site to limit development to three houses. There was an outline planning approval, dated 10 August 1962 which envisaged three detached bungalows with garages, 'sun-worshipping hippos', as Peter called them, sprawling all over the site and demanding that most of the trees be felled. Determined to do better, 'to add to the history of the village, not eliminate it', he sketched four houses, just to prove that they could be fitted in without destroying a tree. Having made the point, but declining to wait through lengthy arguments over the covenant, he settled down to think seriously about three houses, after carefully checking with the local planning authority that there were no further restrictions.

The Aldingtons' purchase, in Margaret's name, was completed on 11 April 1963. It was a late and freezing spring, and May before they could survey the site which was head high with brambles and nettles, but promising primroses, bluebells, narcissi and blossoms. Launching into vigorous attack with machetes, and actually in the process of removing a dead poplar, they were accosted by an architect (one of about a dozen who already lived in

Opposite:
This part of the old orchard reminds us of May 1963 when, released from snowdrifts, the unfettered growth of the previous 16 years tangled gloriously overhead! It was a joyous place for wildlife which we tried to disturb as little as possible, continuing to have bats and dormice until an owl joined us for three years.

Haddenham) who assumed they were developers setting out to clear-fell the site. This was what the village was used to and there were understandable sensitivities. In time the curious became friendly, with neighbourly offerings of tea and cakes, though not a little puzzlement about the repeated appearances of this energetic young couple who started to tend their site as if it were their garden (which of course it was). For, if the truth is told, once they had talked over the plan for the three houses, agreeing that one was to be their own, they were captivated by their building plot, its trees, flowers, old walls and sense of place. Having found a self-confessed missionary zeal, they intended to flout the perennial paradox, that in order to build one must first destroy. Their houses would rise without so much as harming a bluebell or walnut branch whenever possible, and, as their affection blossomed, so it spread to embrace Haddenham itself. They were captivated by the ancient yet lively community, they wanted to become part of it, to become involved.

Right:
Plan diagram showing the layout of houses envisaged in the outline planning permission existing when we bought the site (note that most of the trees in the centre have been ignored).
Far right:
An initial idea for four houses showing that these could be accommodated while still retaining the principal trees and creating a positive relationship with the neighbouring houses on Townside

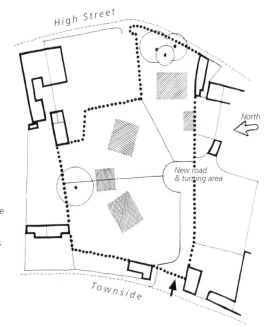

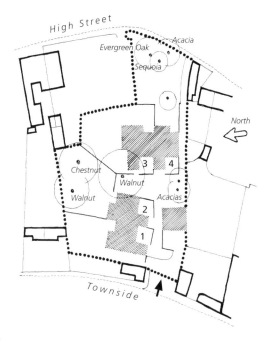

Opposite:
Looking through wichert walls out of and into garden spaces in winter.
Left:
Part of the garden in winter as it is now. This reminds us of the site as it appeared in February 1963 when we first saw it.

Above:
Turn End today

the village

Haddenham is called "the largest village in the Vale of Aylesbury". It is on a secondary road, six miles south-west from Aylesbury, two miles from Thame. The main A418 passes to the north. It is a multi-linear village, with a maze of streets, straggling for almost a mile to link the medieval church of St Mary the Virgin at the south, Church End, to the more mundane Townsend, in the north.

It is also a village with a history of yeoman independence, rather than of aristocratic fiefdom. For centuries it lived well enough on agriculture, until the enclosures of the early nineteenth century deprived smallholders and cottagers of their land. The story of how they re-adjusted their lives, adopting trades and crafts that would provide mutual support, as carpenters, builders, bakers, carters, lace makers and duck breeders, is told by Walter Rose in his memoir, "Good Neighbours", first published in 1949. Rose, from an old Haddenham Quaker family, is in the class of Richard Jefferies and W H Hudson as a writer of fine prose about rural life, and he is now something of a local legend. He is particularly good on the fabric of Haddenham, of which he had a craftsman-carpenter's understanding.

Great avenues of elms once crossed this landscape (though they were finally lost to Dutch elm disease in the 1970s). Plentiful elm and oak had built the big thatched barns and farm steadings, still prominent as outlines in the village, especially in Townside. Around the steadings and lining the village streets are its renowned walls, long spectacular runs of rendered, once thatched, now pantiled, walls. These may be picturesque now, but they were built purely for use: they sheltered everyone, kept in the pigs and ducks, kept out the fox and larger raiders, they protected yards and garden plots and they were the solution to a dozen different demarcation problems, born of the countryman's canny ability to make the best of whatever nature might provide. As Walter Rose

Opposite:
The houses today seen from the village street. The walnut tree in the foreground was transplanted from Turn End's courtyard. (see page 39) No 9 Townside is on the right.

wrote, '*nature had made generous provision for the village… a deep layer of chalk-like mixture was to be found in plenty*' just beneath the soil. This wichert or wichut was an all-purpose building material; it was dug in the autumn, exposed to the frost, then mixed with water and kneaded with straw, and the "masoners", the builders, layered it in chunks on a stone base, using a short and flat-pronged fork. It was left to set after each eighteen inches or so, and built up to the required height as wide, about sixteen-inches wide, walls. The sides were smoothed with a spade, later rendered or roughcast, and the tops thatched for weather protection. With a peculiar poignancy, in view of the story that follows, Walter Rose was lyrical on the result – and he must have written this at about the time of the 1947 Town & Country Planning Act:

'*No town planning scheme hampered their efforts; each man built to his own sweet will until at last the village became a curious maze of walls and narrow ways where often the stranger walks in perplexity even yet*'.[14]

When the Aldingtons arrived in the spring of 1963, Walter Rose had only fairly recently died. His village, as he had well known, was growing and changing even faster than during his lifetime, but it had not lost its spirit. Productive allotments, well-run charities, too many clubs and societies to count and conscientious church and chapel attendances were the evidence of a thriving community. Dr Beeching had closed the railway station, the motorway age had dawned, the M1 was open and the M40 being planned: Frederick Pooley, Buckinghamshire's County Architect and Chief Planning officer, was hatching his great plan to conserve the Chiltern Hills in the south of his county by directing the bulk of development to the north, to the new city of Milton Keynes. Villages in the Vale of Aylesbury in between these poles of conservation and development, were to be judiciously "infilled". Planning in Haddenham was enshrined in a 1958 Town Map, which marked Thame Road, Churchway and Station Road as principal traffic roads, with one or two small areas designated for industry on the fringes of what was predominantly a residential village. There were still many traditional views, as captured in one of John Hookham's drawings for "Good Neighbours" and reproduced above, although modern residents preferred the ghosts of happy hoards of Aylesbury ducks rather than their present company.

Note:
14. Walter Rose, *Good Neighbours. Some Recollections of an English Village and its People, written down by Walter Rose, Author of The Village Carpenter. Drawings by John Hookham. Cambridge University Press, 1949, chapter 4, Village Crafts and Building.*

Left:
Archways have been made in wichert walls at Turn End to link different garden spaces. The urn framed by an arch leads the eye and invites exploration. The rose is 'Climbing Cécile Brunner'.

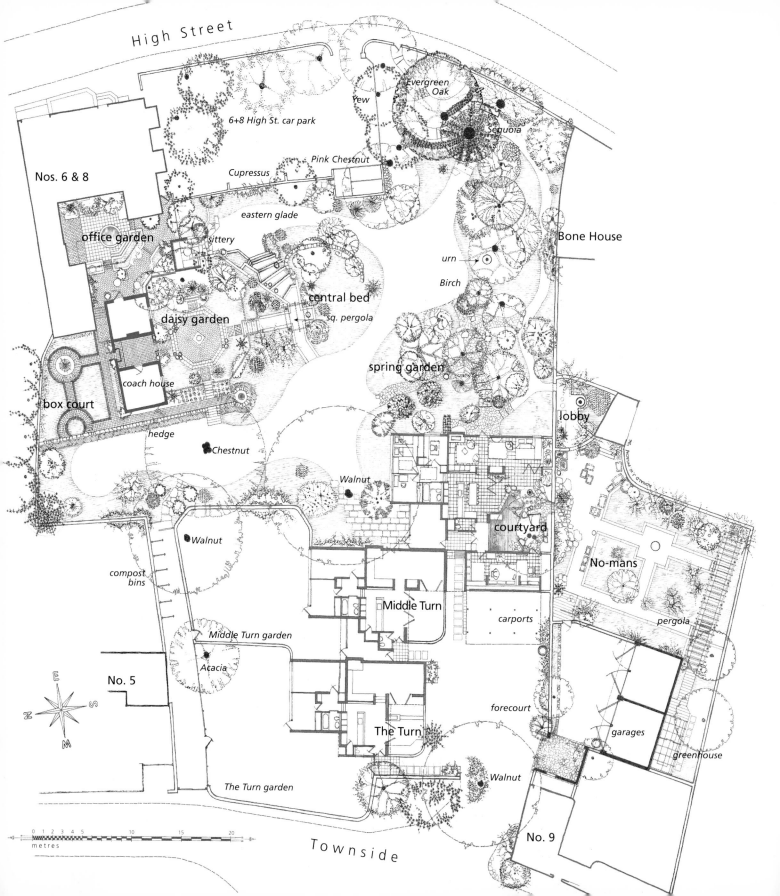

High Street

Nos. 6 & 8

6+8 High St. car park

Yew

Evergreen Oak

Sequoia

Pink Chestnut

Cupressus

Bone House

office garden

eastern glade

sittery

urn

Birch

central bed

daisy garden

sq. pergola

spring garden

coach house

box court

lobby

hedge

Chestnut

Walnut

courtyard

No-mans

Walnut

pergola

compost bins

Middle Turn

carports

Middle Turn garden

Acacia

No. 5

The Turn

forecourt

garages

greenhouse

The Turn garden

Walnut

No. 9

0 1 2 3 4 5   10   15   20
metres

Townside

designing

In that first summer of 1963 the approach to the building site along Townside was through wichert walls and old cottages and barns; there were open fields opposite the site entrance, which was between two small cottages, both only a few feet from the roadway. The sense of a community tightly gathered together, in contrast to the loosely flowing countryside, had not then been diluted by "sprawl", and this togetherness was the tradition that Peter Aldington wanted to emulate with his design.

The three houses were designed in an L-shaped layout in the south-west part of the site, most suited to the prime requirements for sun and privacy. That the only possible entrance for cars was also in this south west corner was both good and bad: good because the intrusion into the site was kept to a minimum, but not so good for the seclusion of the houses. The walled traditions of Haddenham came to the rescue. Each house was to wrap around and enclose an outdoor space, a small court, and these were on the southern sunny side; Turn End's courtyard was to utilise a fragment of old wichert wall on the south boundary, and it would embrace a walnut and some robinias. The walnut was later removed to the entrance court, leaving a hole for the courtyard pool.

Each house was to have three elements, a living area opening onto the sunny courtyard (as at Askett Green), a dining and kitchen area which was the centre of action in the farmhouse tradition, and a quiet and secluded sleeping area. The intensity of tightly grouped cottage roofs was the inspiration for each element to have its own external identity in a single pitched roof, thus completely avoiding any impression of bulkiness. The careful placing of windows, the incorporation of glass doors which became walls, and few full height partitions, ensured that the interiors reflected the changing lights and seasons. Good insulaton and oversized chunkiness – *a more primitive æsthetic*' than conventional bricks –

The plan opposite shows the site as it is today. It was not this extensive when the houses were designed. See diagrams on pages 32 and 66.

dictated the choice of Durox Aerated Blocks, in a basic 18 × 9 inches unit, for the walls. These were to be painted white for interiors, but needed exterior protection, rather in the way of the traditional wichert. The modern interpretation of old Haddenham technique came into play, with exterior roughcast, whitened, then pantiled, the new walls melding with their older neighbours.

In the later part of the summer both the site clearing and design thinking were interrupted with something of a jolt, by the arrival of men and machines on the opposite side of Townside, felling an avenue of magnificent chestnuts as a preliminary to the building of the Dovecote estate. That this development had not been revealed in their searches was bad enough, but the wanton felling of the trees was worse; it was to galvanise other village people, led by Diana Alderson, into a campaign to conserve Haddenham's trees and plant more, and it confirmed Peter's resolve to demonstrate that trees and houses could live together. The architect from the Dovecote development apparently ventured into the Aldingtons' site one day, and on being told that all these trees were staying put, he retorted

'You can't do that in the real world'. This was to become the Turn End battle cry.

The preliminary layouts for the village housing were presented to the Area Planning Officer in Aylesbury on 25 October 1963. A snag materialised over the old bye-law 68, which demanded a minimum of twenty-four feet of open space in front of each house: The Turn and Middle Turn had L-shaped fronts onto their little courts, and Turn End's front door was tucked behind the carport, with the house "front" facing its own courtyard. It was known that bye-law 68 was in the revisionary pipeline, and it was agreed that a letter from Peter, explaining the L-shaped fronts and requesting a waiver for his scheme, would probably overcome any difficulty. The Area Planning Officer, Mr Selby, liked the scheme very much, he went so far as to say he wished for more like it, and he put the matter before the Aylesbury RDC planning committee on 13 November. The Aldingtons were assured that there was unlikely to be any difficulty over the bye-law, the Council would apply for a waiver when permission was granted, and they should submit their planning application. This was done on 1 December 1963.

The Turn and Middle Turn from the gravel forecourt – a public, but private space which allows both vehicles and pedestrians access to all three houses. Curved courtyard walls invite exploration, lead to front doors and reflect the 'soft' character of the indigenous wichert walls. The precise height of these was determined during building to invite the eye while retaining privacy.
Clerestory windows above the front roofs provide sunlight to central bathrooms. Breaking roofs up in this way helps to reduce the apparent scale to one more in harmony with neighbouring cottages.
The two walnuts and a horse chestnut behind Middle Turn are some of the trees we were determined to keep.

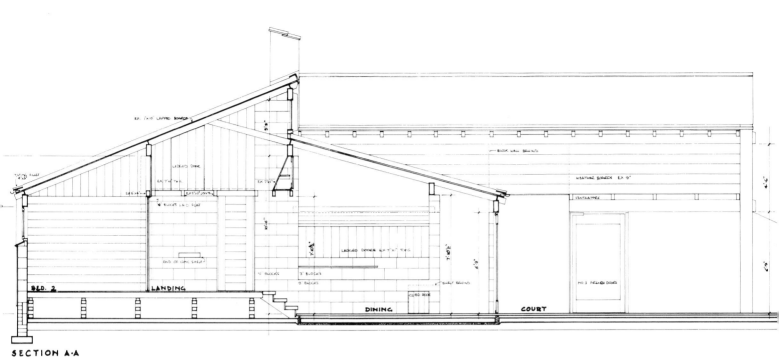

SECTION A·A

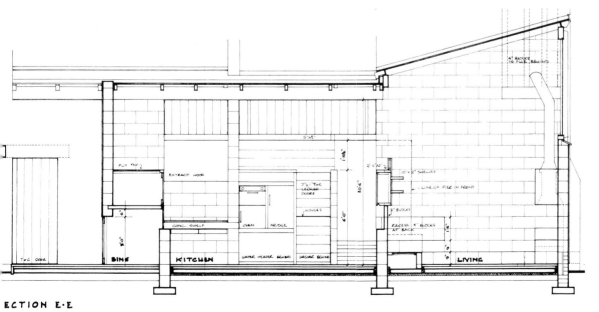

ECTION E·E

Two of the original sectional drawings made while designing. These were drawn at the same time as the plans and are an essential part of the process.

The houses are designed round the dimensions of the principal element of structure, the concrete block. Every block is drawn and each piece of wood is shown.

Cupboards, some of which become walls between different spaces, kitchen fittings and built in seats are all on these drawings, and designed as integral parts of the whole. The houses were built substantially as drawn with only minor variations. See also the detailed drawing on page 52.

planning…

The planning application went swiftly to committee on Wednesday 11 December 1963; under item 525 it was among several approved pending the planning officer's observations, meaning that when he had caught up with his site visits and paperwork, it would be merely administrative.[15] There was a note from the planning officer, querying the ownership of the Townside boundary, but as this presented no problem in the Aldingtons' minds they assumed all would be well, continued finishing Askett Green and turned their attentions to Christmas.

It was therefore something of a shock to open their New Year post and find a letter requesting that the whole scheme be moved back by thirty feet from Townside, to conform with a road improvement (i.e. widening) line, which seemed to have materialised during the festive season. That Townside was not even a "principal traffic road" on the Town Map, that it was seventeen feet wide at the most, tightly bordered by wichert walls and thatched barns, made an improbability of such improvement.[16] That their repeated searches and requests to the local authority for any planning limitations had not revealed any such line drove Peter hotfoot into the area planning office. He was shown (not without some puzzlement) a note from the County Surveyor referring to a 1939 Central Bucks Joint Planning Committee Scheme for all rural districts' village streets to be improved.[17] 1939? But that was another world? Could this outdated notion not be waived out of sight too? Apparently not, or not without reference back to the County Highways Committee who had sanctioned the scheme in the first place. This committee were not to meet until 24 March.

It was still mid-winter and long before any sign of spring the precious planning application for their three houses sank into a black hole of bureaucratic indecision, though no one said anything to the Aldingtons at the time. They appealed to Frederick Pooley, the County Architect (as architect to

Notes:
15. Minutes of Aylesbury RDC Planning Committee, 1963, Buckinghamshire County Archives, County Hall, Aylesbury.
16. 1958 Town Map, Development Plan Sheet no 13, Aylesbury Vale District Council, Planning & Building Control, Exchange Street, Aylesbury.
17. Letter from County Surveyor, 30 January 1964, Turn End microfiche file, Aylesbury Vale District Council.

Architect!) and Planning Officer, and to their MP, John Hall, citing all the good and positive things about their scheme and that no road improvement line had been revealed in their legal searches. John Hall was sympathetic and wanted to help, but the Whitehall correspondence tended to confusion between the waiving of bye-law 68 (where there was no real problem) and the relaxing of the 1939 road improvement line, where the county highways department were standing their ground. It eventually became clear that Frederick Pooley wanted this 1939 curse on village roads removed, and he saw the Aldingtons as a test case. The official line was that there was plenty of room to move the houses back thirty feet (if the applicant felled his trees) and that other applicants were conforming (and felling their trees). That the precious, intense streetscape of Townside was sacrificed in this official reasoning did not seem to matter. When the 24 March finally rolled round,

the County Highways Committee passed the Aldingtons' case to a new Joint Committee on Highways and Planning, which had yet to be appointed, let alone have a date for meeting.[18]

At Askett Green, Margaret and Peter were becoming desperate. Good building weather had arrived, they now knew that Mike and Celia White would be returning at the end of the year to reclaim their house, and they could not afford to be a test case for the removal of the iniquitous building line from Buckinghamshire's village streets. On 5 May 1964, after five months' kicking their heels, they put in an application for one house, Turn End, safely back from any improvement line. The application was approved on 13 May, minute 983, planning permission came through on 27 May and was confirmed on 1 June. But, both financially and ideologically, it was a tremendous gamble.

A section through the site looking to the north, from Townside on the left, through the forecourt looking towards The Turn and Middle Turn; the carport; Turn End studio, courtyard and living room; down Turn End garden past the stoneware urn, the sequoia and evergreen oak to High Street on the right.

Note:
18. 1964 Minutes of County Planning and County Highways Committees, Buckinghamshire County Archives.

RJWW 98

building

Starting on the site was celebrated with the purchase of a Winget concrete mixer with a Villiers engine for £105 and a new builder's barrow. A local contractor helped move the topsoil aside and relocate the walnut to the entrance court; a neighbour, Ken Plested, resting from his night-job as a magician, taught the Aldingtons the comparatively effortless way of cleaving clay with a mattock, and helped them dig the foundations. At 9.45 a.m. on 13 June the first Premix concrete lorry arrived.

The first load of Durox blocks for the walls came on 21 July, more loads following regularly. Sometimes the blocks were so fresh from the oven that they were too hot to handle; everything was unloaded by hand. Electricity came to the site in early August. The walls were rising so well that the first delivery of timber was anticipated in early September. These ten by five inch roof beams of Canadian Douglas Fir, some forty feet long, all beautifully finished, were vulnerable to every mark. The experience of Askett Green had taught that every piece had to be protected with plastic. For the roof boards Dolton Bournes and Dolton of High Wycombe had found them a parcel of Siberian redwood planks, eleven inches wide, an inch thick, which was sufficient for Turn End's roof and the front door. These redwood planks went on to rafters supported by the Douglas Fir beams, then the roof was layered with felt, expanded polystyrene insulation, spacers, sarking felt, and finally tiling battens and Redland Delta terracotta tiles. These were concrete tiles, carefully chosen modern technology, but having the "feel" and quality of clay pantiles: they have proved immensely durable and are beautiful in their own right. Nineteen hundred tiles cost just over £160 in September 1964.

In that late summer and into autumn, when at least the weather was on their side, and it remained gloriously fine, the Aldingtons worked single-mindedly on their house. Almost at the

moment the timber arrived, their hoped-for carpenters found another priority, so Peter gave up working at the Timber Research and Development Association, and became his own carpenter. Margaret, who worked on site full time from the beginning, has calculated that they handled some 700 tons of concrete between them, let alone the timber, in fact everything that made their house; it was a salutary bonding process. They remember with gratitude the cups of tea, with scones on Sundays, shyly handed over the wall of no. 9 Townside by a remarkable lady was to become the first of many friends.

That autumn the floor tiles were laid by another colourful craftsman, A.W.H. Saville, known as "Jimmy". He made a work of art with the big heavy, twelve inches square, nearly two inches thick, terracotta quarries which are the glory of the kitchen, dining and living areas and the courtyard. These were a wonderful find, from Stanley Brothers of Nuneaton, who had them as a stock pile of rejects. The first load of 200, costing £11.11s. 8d were delivered in November, and in the end the Aldingtons bought the whole stock which was enough for all three houses.

The Aldingtons moved into their home after Christmas. "Into" was not quite right word, for though they were roofed and partly floored, the window spaces sheeted and polythened from the worst elements, their sleeping bags were in the one bedroom with floorboards, and the primus stove was in the other, between the floor joists.

Raw concrete blocks are not easy to visualise as a backdrop to living. The concrete seat in the upper picture is now at the head of the dining table. (see also page 12)
Top photo Peter Aldington

Far left:
Summer 1964, original wichert wall and acacia trees left standing. (see page 18) Sequoia, holm oak and acacia on High Street boundary beyond apple trees; pivotal walnut extreme left.
Left:
Summer 1964, Turn End bedrooms. (see also page 94) Middle Turn, not yet started, will wrap round the pivotal walnut. Note proximity of this to buildings.

Far left:
Late summer 1964, Turn End's Douglas Fir beams protected from weather and dirty hands! Apart from paint on blockwork and lacquer on timber every thing is as it now appears in the house.
Left:
Summer 1965, foundations of Middle Turn, shell of Turn End's bedrooms and workshop in background.
L to R: Colin Stillwell, Roger Smith, Ken Plested, Margaret.

Far left, above:
Autumn 1965, Peter working on the roof of Middle Turn and The Turn.
Far left, below:
Late summer 1965, Middle Turn to roof level, The Turn beginning; car port and transplanted walnut in place. This is a similar view to...
Left:
The entrance court to all three houses as it is today. The transplanted walnut is nearly as big as its parent behind the roof!

All photos this page except bottom right Peter Aldington.

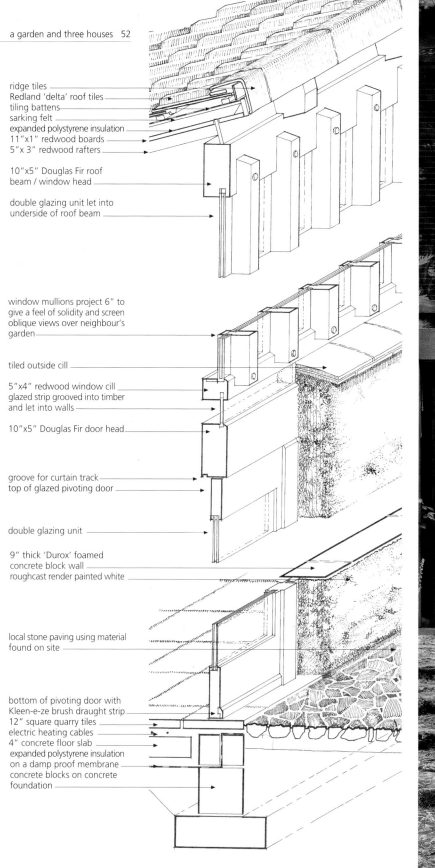

ridge tiles
Redland 'delta' roof tiles
tiling battens
sarking felt
expanded polystyrene insulation
11"x1" redwood boards
5"x 3" redwood rafters

10"x5" Douglas Fir roof
beam / window head

double glazing unit let into
underside of roof beam

window mullions project 6" to
give a feel of solidity and screen
oblique views over neighbour's
garden

tiled outside cill

5"x4" redwood window cill
glazed strip grooved into timber
and let into walls

10"x5" Douglas Fir door head

groove for curtain track
top of glazed pivoting door

double glazing unit

9" thick 'Durox' foamed
concrete block wall
roughcast render painted white

local stone paving using material
found on site

bottom of pivoting door with
Kleen-e-ze brush draught strip
12" square quarry tiles
electric heating cables
4" concrete floor slab
expanded polystyrene insulation
on a damp proof membrane
concrete blocks on concrete
foundation

The anatomy of a window.
This pivoting door and upper
window are the most
dominant features on the
spring garden side of the
house. The drawing and
photograph, far left, illustrate
the complexity of detail
necessary to achieve apparent
simplicity. The photograph this
page shows the door in early
summer.

…and unplanning

Over a year had now passed since the original planning application for the three houses, and something of the events that caused this delay can be discovered from the local authority archives. In the new year of 1964, when the road improvement line on Townside had emerged like the spectre of seasonal ill-will, the major topic of conversation amongst planners and architects was Colin Buchanan's Traffic in Towns report, predicting the demolition of historic Britain to satisfy the motor car. All highway authorities had been instructed to look out their provisions, and presumably this was how the 1939 scheme came to light: they were also to set up joint highways and planning committees, which Buckinghamshire County Council sanctioned at their meeting on 13 January 1964. On 24 March the County Highways Committee lobbed the Aldingtons' application to this new joint committee, the Buchanan Committee as it was now called, which came into being in the summer. Their recorded deliberations are elusive, but it seems unlikely that they gave a verdict on the Aldingtons' application. Perhaps the County Planning Committee had remembered the village housing in Haddenham? No, they were busy with Milton Keynes and the new council headquarters in Aylesbury, now known as Pooley's Palace. Did the Highways Committee remember? No, they were busy with the M40 and had a staffing shortfall of over forty in the department, which may have had something to do with the oversight.[19]

The Aldingtons' scheme was nobody's concern: only John Hall had persevered, and finally stung Frederick Pooley into telephoning Margaret. He was charming but petulant over John Hall's sixth letter on the subject. *'Perhaps you should have answered the previous five'*, quipped Margaret; an explanatory meeting followed,[20] but the Aldingtons felt none the wiser. Frederick Pooley's parting advice was *'I should appeal if I were you'*. They had already considered this, so the appeal was lodged on 19 August 1964, on the grounds

Opposite:
Evening sunlight on Turn End seen from No-mans in late spring. This part of the garden was made in the early 1980s on what used to be part of 16 High Street (see text, page 73). The frontispiece shows the same view in summer, page 44 in winter.

Notes:
19. County Planning and County Highways Committee Minutes as before; Buchanan Committee (Traffic in Towns sub-Committee) Matters in 1964/65 published Buckinghamshire County Council Papers, County Reference Library, County Hall, Aylesbury.
20. Frederick Pooley to John Hall, letter 5 August 1964, Turn End microfiche file, Aylesbury Vale District Council.

of non-determination of their application of
1 December 1963.

The ensuing correspondence between Whitehall
and Aylesbury reiterated the well worn phrases:
that Townside (all of seventeen feet wide) was
important for traffic, that the appellant had plenty
of room to move his houses back by thirty feet (if
he felled his trees) and others had acquiesced (and
felled their trees). Unknown to the Aldingtons, the
Clerk to Buckinghamshire County Council had
written to the chief officers on 15 September 1964
urging a decision on the road improvement policy
as he felt it would be 'difficult to justify on pure
highway grounds' at any public inquiry.[21]

The Aldingtons approached the Royal Institute of
British Architects, who referred them to Lord Esher,
Chairman of their Town Planning Committee, a
Senior Vice-President and a Member of the Royal
Fine Art Commission. Lord Esher visited the site
immediately, and concurred 'unreservedly' with
Peter's frustrations: 'his strong feelings seem to me
to have every justification', he wrote, 'it is perfectly
true that a relaxation for Mr Aldington could be
quoted as a precedent for others – and so it
should be. There must always be cases where
particular site conditions, the preservation of
trees... the preservation of old walls... fully justify
such relaxation and these should be judged on
their merits'. And, as for quoting amenity in
defence of a road improvement line, it was just
such lines 'systematically enforced' that were so
largely responsible 'for the disastrous failure of our
generation to build village housing that has a
satisfactory relation with our old villages'.

Lord Esher's report was seen by everyone
concerned by early December. The file languished
through another Christmas, Whitehall asked the
County Council what was happening on 18
February 1965, and on 11 March the Clerk
responded, saying that the Council's "internal
procedures" had changed with regard to road

Note:
21. Clerk of the County
Council to County Surveyor
and County Planning Officer,
letter 15 September 1964,
Turn End microfiche file,
Aylesbury Vale D C.

improvement lines. These were now a planning
matter (i.e. County Planning Officer Pooley
had won) and at their meeting on 8 March the
County Planning Committee had agreed that
Mr Aldington's 'was an imaginative scheme' and
that the road improvement line should be relaxed
to allow it to be built, provided that the
Aldingtons' appeal was withdrawn. Margaret was
sent a copy of this letter, with a note from the
Clerk, 'no doubt if you were to write to the
Ministry agreeing to the course I suggest the
matter could be quickly resolved'. Was there no
humanity, no well-mannered concern, no apology,
that for fifteen months their future, their savings,
their hopes and ideals, had been held to ransom
by bickering officials and outdated policies? No, of
course not. Margaret did as she was asked, and
the planning permission for the village housing
scheme was finally granted on 18 March 1965.

Opposite:
The site held many secrets and
we tried to keep this quality by
making a garden of secret
places
Left:
Turn End's garden door opens
onto a spring woodland
garden. The resolution of the
planning difficulties enabled us
to save these trees and make
them part of a new whole.
These vignettes of a garden
yet to be made in 1964 are
enhanced by Svend Bayer and
Monica Young stoneware pots.

a home and half a garden

Despite feeling completely in the dark about the Aylesbury machinations as to their fate, the Aldingtons had just kept on building Turn End. The luxury of glass gradually replaced polythene sheets; the most difficult job was the big clerestory window high up in the living room wall, which was finally glazed in the freezing dark of the small hours of a February morning. More comfortly "the best tradesman they knew", George Williams of Bledlow, worked steadily and carefully through the electrical wiring, adapting his skill to Peter's unconventional demands.

The fixtures and fittings for Turn End, for which every well-thumbed and tattered original delivery docket has been carefully kept, reveal a fascinating roll call of a thriving British building supply industry of the sixties: a Sissons stainless steel sink and trough for the kitchen, a Creda cooker and Hotpoint refrigerator, Adamsez lavatories and basins, Barking Brassware taps, a Permutit water softener, Kleeneze draught excluders, Rotaflex lighting, Henderson and Hill Aldam sliding door gear, Plyglass double glazing, Freeman's Cementone interior flat finish for the walls, Abercorn clear satin lacquer for the wood, and Dryad and Allgoods in the Euston Road for door furniture, locks and latches. The big $3/8$ inch thick polished plate glass for the wall overlooking the courtyard was a special delivery from James Clark & Eaton at Oxford. This cost £48 in 1965; it has been re-quoted at £1,227 in early 1998.

The Aldingtons were able to secure the shell of their house and escape to Scotland for a spring holiday. On their return they advertised for some Oxford student labour to start work on the other two houses. The willing victims were both undergraduates at Wadham College, Roger Smith and Colin Stillwell; they remember the summer camp atmosphere, camping in the partly-finished Turn End and picnicking in the wild garden in glorious summer weather, which lightened the labouring.

Opposite:
This picture through the glass over the pond illustrates better than many the unity of inside and outside spaces. The illusion is fostered by the absence of a window frame; the glass is contained within render wrapping round the blockwork and is housed in slots in the roof beam and floor.

Spring 1965. Turn End kitchen, in use despite being a building site. Note the curtain used to screen the bathroom and a newly ironed shirt airing! Photo Peter Aldington

The garden, really the remnant of old orchard, had flowered riotously with spring flowers, amidst a carpet of ivy and ground elder. Enough old apple and pear trees remained to make the area immediately outside the garden door into a potential spring woodland garden. Beyond, there was a more open, sunny space, which natural logic seemed to decree 'should be summer orientated, both in contrast to the woodland and as a reaction to its more open character'. The beginnings of a summer flower border were made against what was then the eastern site boundary, but as yet there was neither money nor momentum to fill it. The garden's soil was exhibiting temperamental extremes, baked and cracked in dry weather, running mud in the wet, so bales of straw and manure were delivered to implement a rigorous composting and mulching regime. An old straight path of concrete, some former gardener's barrow route, was found running parallel to the south wall. Whenever additional exercise was needed this was broken up and used as a hardcore base for the present meandering shady path.

In early September Peter bought himself a present of a load of rocks for the courtyard. The hole vacated by the walnut tree (now in the entrance court) was concreted and rendered and became a successful pool, with the rocks carefully arranged around and beneath the robinia. A streak of gardening independence was asserted here, for he feels certain that his rock garden reading had forbidden pools beneath trees, but he decided to trade the continual leaf clearing of the pool for its reflected sparkles and shadows, and the pleasures of living in a carpet-close relationship with water.

There was a modest celebration for Christmas Day 1965 in the far from complete Turn End, despite some table construction that had to be put in hand before eating lunch! It must have been hard to appreciate, but there were reasons for celebrating; for once they had eased themselves out of their building purdah, the Aldingtons had found friends, and even admirers. The many who were frankly dubious about the young self-builders and their concrete, wood and glass house, came back and admitted that they thought Turn End was beautiful. Some of them came with the ultimate accolade of wanting a similar building for themselves.[22] Others realised that the Aldingtons shared their long-held concerns over the fate of Haddenham's trees and the threat to widen village streets: this was to lead to the founding of the Haddenham Village Society, with Reg Carslake as the first Chairmam, and Margaret as the first Secretary.

Note:
22. Peter Aldington's early works locally include an addition at Fort End for Mr and Mrs Carslake, Chinnor Surgery for Dr Reedy and partners, a house at Prestwood for Mr and Mrs Quilter and Diggs Field for Miss Diana Alderson.

The kitchen today. Visually this is one of our favourite corners. The cloakroom wall on the left stopping short of the roof and light from the porch window behind (see also page 77) provide a feeling of spaciousness to what is just a one metre wide floor space.

The strong geometry of the house is counterpointed by the now mature garden. This area still reminds us of summer picnics with Colin and Roger while continuing to build the other two houses.

An early photograph by
Richard Einzig shows the
newly completed Turn End
courtyard garden. We carried
the rocks for this our 'first'
garden through a nearly
finished house! In the picture
Peter is talking to Renate
Einzig.
Compare this with the
courtyard today on pages
42 & 43.
Photo Richard Einzig/Arcaid

haddenham specific

This is the architect's term, meaning that his village housing could not have been built anywhere else, that the houses grew out of their surroundings and expressed the integrity of his concept. The planning threat to the whole scheme had loomed as a potential disaster simply because the three houses together were an architectural entity. Turn End alone, which from the Townside entrance appears as an elegantly reclusive pantiled roof amongst leafery, was only part of the picture. As Middle Turn and The Turn neared completion in the spring of 1967 the whole became apparent. They are projected forward, as the stem of a reverse ell, and their white roughcast walls ripple towards the roadside, picking up the walled character of Townside.

There was a small hitch in the completeness because of a condemned cottage, no. 7 Townside, adjoining The Turn. This was resolved on 31 August 1967 with the reluctantly agreed demolition of the cottage, and the purchase for £100 of a strip of land which extended The Turn's garden and added a garden deliveries' entrance and "compostery" area north of Middle Turn and The Turn's garden walls. The response to the disappearance of no. 7 was to build a new wall to protect the entrance: it was the traditional Haddenham response, and brings a strong sense of arrival to the entrance court. Whatever the weather, howling gale or searing heat, arrival is a silent ushering into the dappled shade of the walnut and the sheltering court, where roses, clematis, euphorbias and forsythia extol their time-honoured virtues and soothe away the hostility of city and motorway. The first impression of the village housing, now completed, is of unobtrusive well-mannered well-being, the essentials of traditional village England.

In July 1967 the lease of Middle Turn was sold to John and Betty Landon. At that time the houses were simply nos. 1, 2 and 3 The Turn – which had referred to the turn around in planning fortunes – and it was the Landons' desire for a house name that led to the christening of The Turn, Middle Turn and Turn End.

Above:
The entrance adapted after the demolition of no 7 Townside. See text this page.

Opposite:
Entrances are events. Here, Middle Turn's front door is flanked by a curved courtyard wall and a planting box, inviting entry. The timber letter-box is below a small 'peep' window and there is a shelf for resting parcels or milk bottles. The house floor projects to meet the visitor and form a step. Three paving slabs as stepping stones in the gravel make a transition between forecourt and house.

That John and Betty Landon have been happily in Middle Turn for over thirty years is perhaps the best testimony to the success of Peter's *'neighbourliness with privacy'* design philosophy. Each house has complete privacy within itself and its garden spaces, and yet the villager's instinct for neighbours (and the occasional cup of milk or borrowed matches) is fulfilled without any unwitting intrusion. However, there was a serendipity about the Landons' arrival, and it would be useless to pretend that the Aldingtons were not apprehensive, back in 1967, about the fate of the third house, The Turn. All was resolved the following year: John Creaser, whom Peter had met in the RAF, was English Fellow at Mansfield College and living in a Victorian terrace house in Oxford with his wife Hazel, who was taking a teaching post in Thame in September 1968. Peter put two and two together and the Creasers were delighted to move into The Turn. They loved the efficient use of space, the abundance of light, the warmth of the wood, and how the small court gave them continual opportunities for living outdoors. Even though they outgrew The Turn, Hazel Creaser recalls that *'visually it was a house I would never have left'*.

In 1968 the three carport spaces and the entrance court for parking were fairly generous provision, but it was agreed that some garages would be provided. The Aldingtons had been able to buy, in September 1967, the small wichert-walled no. 9 Townside, on the south of the entrance, for just over the district valuer's figure of £2,000 because it was only three feet from the roadway and thus blighted by the road improvement line. The land behind the cottage allowed almost enough space for the garages; this land abutted the garden of no.16 High Street which fortunately had become available, with tenants, in November 1967. Planning permission for the garages was received at the end of 1969, and it came with the news that the road improvement line had been vanquished, so no. 9 Townside was reprieved, re-furbished with the help of a grant, and was to become the Turn End gardener's cottage.

The ill wind was changing to a benevolent breeze, but not without financial pain. The sale of Middle Turn and The Turn had put the Aldingtons' finances into the black, but the necessity of buying no.16 High Street took them into the red again.

Right:
Plan diagram showing the houses as finally planned on the site bought in 1963. The position of the entrance was determined by the gap between 7 and 9 Townside. Most of the principal trees have been incorporated.
Far right:
Heavy dotted lines define the boundaries as they are today. Note the wall which replaced 7 Townside and the transplanted walnut in the entrance. Garages have been built on part of the garden of 16 High Street and the garden at Turn End is enlarged by the addition of land from 6 and 8 High Street.

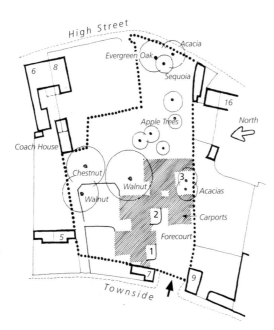

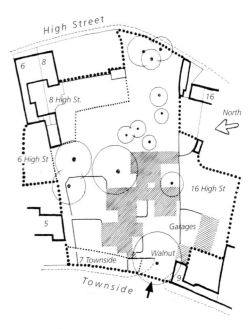

Left:
A view down Townside, nos. 3 and 5 are on the left and 9 right. The garden wall of the demolished no. 7 forms the roadside boundary of The Turn. A new wall protects and defines the entrance court.
Photo Peter Aldington

John Landon and Margaret assist a tree moving specialist with the ash.
Photo Peter Aldington

Looking into the entrance court from across Townside, flanked by no. 9 with High Street houses beyond. The ash tree in the foreground was retrieved from overcrowding at the bottom of Turn End's garden. (above)

the garden grows

The Wadham undergraduates, Roger Smith and Colin Stillwell, who had worked on The Turn and Middle Turn, graduated in 1967. Roger, who was job-hunting, returned in August and worked through the autumn, making the really positive start on the garden. Building the houses had demanded such intense concentration of efforts, that it was with some surprise that he observed the revelation of Peter's serious gardening ambitions and his careful design processes. Except for a few rough sketches, this was not design on paper, but garden making '*by wandering around with canes and drawing shapes full size on the ground*' to set out the margins of the spring woodland, the summer glade and its borders. It was both an exact and evolving process, and despite the changing map, Roger cleared the ground elder and perennial weeds by hand and fork, and planted masses of bulbs.

Left to his own devices, Peter allowed himself '*a willingness to change and move things*'; he studied and adjusted shapes through differing lights and seasons until he was satisfied, and though for several years many of the plants could have done with wheels, the important focus plantings eventually came to rest. This was the same imagining of spaces that had created the houses; his love of materials prompted a sculptural satisfaction in manipulating green forms, the masses of plants and voids of lawn meandered in his mind, and were finally fixed on the ground. In this way the sunny, central glade, the magnetic counter-point to Turn End's dining table was created during 1968.

At the end of that year, knowing that permission had been granted for two houses east of the garden fence, on land adjoining no. 8 High Street, the Aldingtons bought this property. Aided by an improvement grant, the house was converted to flats, with a car park on High Street, leaving a whole new addition to Turn End's garden, with some stately cupressus and the former coach house.

Opposite:
The glade from the haven of the horse chestnut. The gravel path left/centre leads to the square pergola and sequence of more formal gardens. Much of this grass area was originally infested with pernicious weeds like coltsfoot and bindweed, necessitating thorough and careful digging and in some cases, sieving!

Dawn Meadows in the daisy garden. Here the underlying rock stratum was so near the surface that we had to use a mechanical hammer to enable it to be cultivated. The rear wall of the coach house was pierced with an archway to link this garden with the little court and office garden beyond.

Steps up from the daisy garden to the square pergola.

The fence behind the flower border could go, and the sun-loving perennials were liberated into a central, pivotal bed. The grass curled down the slope and behind the flowers, making a secondary, secluded glade beside the new east boundary.

Peter discussed a partnership with John Craig during 1969 and the Aldington+Craig architectural practice came into being on 1 January 1970. John and Pauline Craig bought no.16 High Street to the south of Turn End's garden, but the Aldingtons retained half of no.16's garden, which was a rectangular plot abutting their garage court. This plot was christened No-mans, because for a time there was no connection with the rest of the garden.

The following year, 1971, Turn End was re-mortgaged to enable the rest of Freeman Clarke's big Victorian house, no. 6 High Street, to be bought as a practice office. This yielded a treasure trove of old bakery fittings and floorings and a small space north of the coach house, all for Turn End's garden.

At this point Peter acknowledges a consciously borrowed garden idea: he had long admired a garden in the village which had a small, open building in the centre, giving a vista through it, with contrasting garden views. The coach house became his see-through garden building. To set up the vista he cut a narrow path through the flowers of the pink and blue central bed to the point of seeing-through and, to screen "the tallest house in Haddenham", built a simple 6 feet square pergola of rough poles, planted with roses and purple-leaved vine. The pergola also launched the vista, down a few steps into the paved octagon known as the Daisy garden, through the coach house to the tiny court beyond. The visual conclusion is the bakery's cast iron dough mixing bowl set in a circle of deeply-etched floor blocks from the old stable. The domestic nature of the little court suggested it might be an ornamental vegetable garden, but this

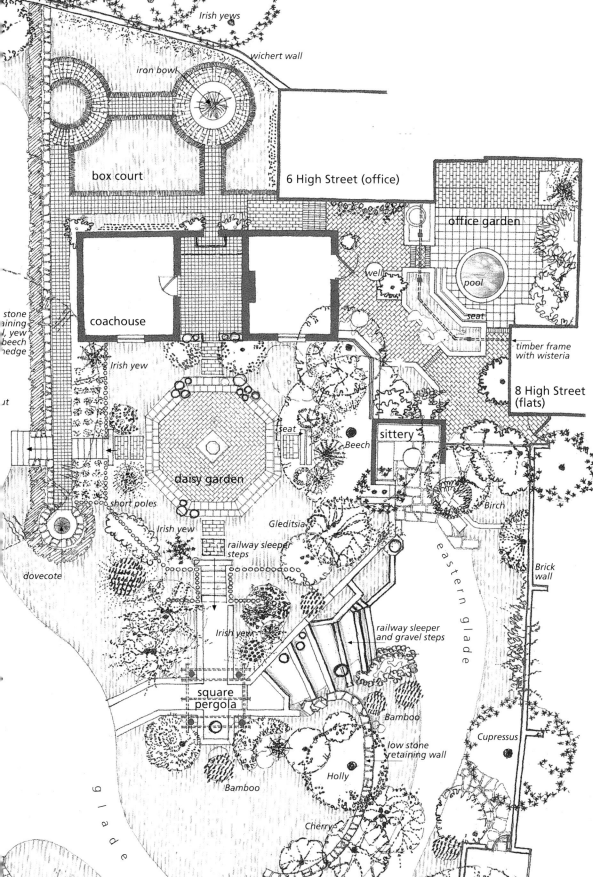

Irish yews

wichert wall

iron bowl

box court

6 High Street (office)

coachouse

stone
aining
, yew
beech
edge

Irish yew

dovecote

Irish yew

daisy garden

seat

short poles

Irish yew

Gleditsia

railway sleeper
steps

Irish yew

square
pergola

Bamboo

Bamboo

Holly

Cherry

glade

office garden

well

pool

seat

timber frame
with wisteria

8 High Street
(flats)

sittery

Beech

Birch

Brick
wall

eastern glade

railway sleeper
and gravel steps

low stone
retaining wall

Cupressus

Unlike most of the garden, this series of garden 'rooms' was designed on the drawing board, and we made them between 1970 and 1976.

The sequence starts at the square pegola which marks the junction with the route from the original glade to the newer eastern glade. The axis from this pergola runs through the daisy garden and the open part of the old coach house to the large cast iron dough mixing bowl in the box court. A cross axis is suggested by the timber seat in the daisy garden and a corresponding gap in the hedge opposite, leading to the area under the chestnut tree.

In contrast to these spaces the office garden does not lie on a route and is non-axial. This has enabled it to be more abstract in layout and adopt forms which suggest and encourage pause and reflection rather than movement. The south side of this garden is bounded by the high rear wall of the 'sittery' which terminates the eastern glade and is the focus of a quiet secluded place.

Most of the materials used to make the gardens were salvaged. Various kinds of blue-black paving brick are from 6 High Street and the large tiles round the octagon in the daisy garden are old fire-clay liners from the bread oven.

The seat in the daisy garden

The office garden from the steps. Imported lime free soil enables rhododendrons to thrive. *Hydrangea petiolaris* and *Magnolia grandiflora* are on the walls of 8 High street with *Wisteria floribunda* 'Macrobotrys' on the timber framework. Materials used here were largely salvaged from 6 and 8 High street.

The daisy garden seen from inside the coach house in winter and summer. Doors were removed from this opening and low walls built to emphasise the vista terminated by the square pergola and an urn by Svend Bayer.

brush with fashion materialised only for a few seasons, and it became primly hedged with box, filled with annual beddings of a single, vivid colour.

At the east end of this box court is a tiny, stepped doorway, next to the former stable boy's bothy, which leads into the quiet water court, made as the practice office garden. Loads of lime free soil were imported into the raised beds for growing small rhododendrons, camellias, heaths, a skimmia or two, with a delicate carpeting of tellima, ferns, ivies and wood anemones. The biggest plants in this small space are a fig, the *Magnolia grandiflora* on the red brick house wall, and a *Wisteria floribunda* 'Macrobotrys', with extra-long racemes, grown on timber arches. The architectural practice "lived" here from 1979 to 1986; the court will always be maintained as part of Turn End's garden, and it contributes a variation in mood – it is cloistered, often damp and grotto-like, with only the sputter of water bubbling in the pool to break the quiet.

On the opposite side of the garden, the sunny south, the problem of access to No-mans was

solved by acquiring a tiny wedge of land from each of the two properties between Turn End's boundary and no. 16 High Street. The resulting triangular lobby, the smallest of all the garden's spaces, is home to three of the largest plants, the roses 'Climbing Cécile Brunner' and 'Félicité et Perpétue' and a giant bamboo.

This shady, scented, overplanted lobby leads directly into the sunlight of No-mans, a blank ground on which a formal garden was made in the early 1980s. It has an architecturally disciplined plan of straight lines and accurate geometry, with raised beds edged with a double layer of sleepers, allowing a much-needed depth of soil in a usually dry garden. Old railway sleepers have been used elsewhere in the garden, but here their qualities are particularly well displayed: as relatively cheap and available wood for outdoor use, they conform to the "chunky" æsthetic of the beams inside the houses. But perhaps there is an extra satisfaction also, which will be appreciated by anyone who thinks fondly of Britain's railway past, for sleepers draped in lavender and rock roses are as poignant a tribute as Flanders and Swann's *Slow Train*.

Below:
Old railway sleepers

Right and opposite:
This 'shady scented over-planted lobby' connects the main garden to No-mans through arches formed in the wichert walls. A large bamboo (*Fargesia murielæ*) and Rose 'Félicité et Perpétue' rampage. A sequence of three contrasting spaces

turn end spectacular

For all it had undeniably grown on its Haddenham roots, visitors to the completed village housing could be forgiven for divining an oriental influence. The entrance court, framed in white walls and pantiled roofs, the pale ground of crushed stone exuding sunlight, the dappled shade of the solitary walnut tree and the deep shadows in the clefts of the buildings, can all evoke images of courtyards in Suchow or Zen gardens. The plants – kerria, wisteria, *Hydrangea petiolaris*, the forsythia branch against the sky, have similar connections. The oriental regard for plants and scenery, the love of symbolic objects and asymmetry, have seeped into modern architecture and design, and their subtle employment here is perhaps the first of Turn End's allurements. There is intrigue. Where is the front door? How do we gain entry?

Three modest lines of paving direct to the three entrances; the way into Turn End is in the far corner down a tunnel of roughcast, which upon close encounter is irresistible to the touch, is it not really the chunkiest cottage cheese? Only traditional "throwing", a cruel and exhausting exercise, produces this tactile urging. On the right is the front door, made of those precious eleven-inches wide redwood boards; it is in fact a double door, and the wider "half" swings to a light touch on the bronze latch. Inside is a momentary, conventional assurance, an enormous expanse of matting large enough for six or seven to stamp their feet together. But then the horizon dissolves, shimmering into blues and greens, with the sparkle of water half seen through a gauzy curtain. The door has swung to the right, and indicates a turn to the left. Albeit impolite, some expression of wonder is unstoppable. The narrowish vista floored in large terracotta tiles, lit from the right by the inner courtyard, sweeps past a neat row of Eames chairs to the luminescent rectangle of the garden door. There it is softened by leaves and shadows and comes to rest on a sublimely beautiful stoneware urn, set in the shade of elderly, blossoming apple trees. This impression can appear

Opposite:
Turn End's entrance with carports to right of the low wall. The small window lights a corner of the kitchen, glass louvres the cloakroom. The small door hides refuse sacks under a chute. Concrete paving slabs in the forecourt gravel lead through a covered way to the door step in the light beyond, with a turn right to Turn End's front door. (see page 82)
Rose 'Mermaid', *Clematis montana*, and *Lonicera halliana* are underplanted with bergenias and wild asters.

in a hundred guises, according to the season, weather or time of day; at vivid moments, perhaps in the slanting sun of October, with golden leaves and roseate orbs of apples, it can assume a filmic quality, as though the house and garden are conspiring to star in their own spectacular home movie.

It is only a few steps from the front door to the heart of the house. The Eames chairs are lined, four by four, at the long table of blonde polished sycamore. Visitors for meals are invited to choose to look inwards, or outwards: the cook or casual brewer of tea at the kitchen workbench has the optimum position, everything within reach and a view of the garden courtyard. This also has terracotta floor tiles, and the wide glazed doors fold back to make it a fine weather extension to the living area: in all weathers it is fascinatingly picturesque, with pool and goldfish, white water iris, water buttercup and the umbrella plant, *Peltiphyllum peltatum*, all at the feet of the lofty, leaning robinia, its double trunk bobbled and twisted into patterns like an Aran sleeve.

Le Corbusier wrote of his ideal for living – *'that the horizon is present every minute in life'*, and it is worth testing this out, perhaps from the vantage point of the kitchen sink.[23] A small window over the rubbish chute watches the approach to the front door from the entrance court, straight ahead is the courtyard, upwards the sky and a variety of roofs, and through the arch in the wichert wall are the flowers of No-mans' sunny beds. A few steps from the sink and these horizons will shift and new ones come into play: past the sleeping black cat on the bed an enormous *Monstera deliciosa* basks in its own patch of sunlight, through the garden door is the spring woodland, and up high, through the big clerestory above the living room fireplace, the branches wave against the sky. Finally, at the rear of the cave-like sequence of landing and bedrooms are horizontal windows framing the leafy glade beneath the horse

chestnut tree. This constant interweaving of indoors and outdoors reflects the very structure of the house: the block walls are simply whitened as the backdrop to pictures and hanging rugs, the same walls have been stopped or sliced off to form shelves and seats, and support the roof beams. The beams themselves spawn partitions and balconies. This structural self-expression, lightly adorned with beloved ornaments, books and other valued possessions, is the epitome of modern architecture, bringing security with comfort, integrity with warmth.

From the kitchen the summer flowers of No-mans beckon; it is just across the courtyard, through the arch in the wichert wall, to the most intensively planted of Turn End's gardens. There are many and changing treasures: self-set hellebore seedlings, violas and horned poppies are allowed in the gravel, and nestle at the feet of deep purple bearded irises which thrive in the raised beds. Here are sun-lovers: lavenders, cheiranthus, alliums, verbascums, cistus and rock-roses, potentillas penstemons, pinks and hardy geraniums. There is space enough for tall grasses, lavatera and asphodel. Clustered outside the arch are kitchen herbs, chives, thymes and sages, with stone sinks holding alpines, especially saxifrages, and a large collection of terracotta dishes and trays of sempervivums – over fifty different varieties.

The retreat from the sun of No-mans, which is sometimes a relief, is via the lobby hung with roses and into the shade of the main garden. A gravel path meanders along the southern perimeter of the garden, a secret path smelling of moss and damp gravel keeping company with apple branches, rose fronds and a curtain of *Forsythia suspensa sieboldii* that hangs on the wall. The path ends at a footgate onto High Street; beside the gate is a hole in the ground, which some visitors correctly identify as a dairy. The hole was dug down to bed rock, with stone steps down to where the churns of milk stood in ground water to

Note:
23. Le Corbusier and Francois de Pierrefeu, *The Home of Man*, Architectural Press, 1948, p. 114

keep cool. Main drainage has spirited the water away, but two of the garden's biggest trees, the evergreen oak and a sequoia, still cast deep, cool shade.

From the sequoia the grass rolls gently upwards and westwards as the sunny glade. It laps to the left, where the stoneware urn sits serenely amongst ferns, ligularias, hostas and rheums; it laps to the right into the eastern glade; it carries on its sinuously wide middle way, to the pink and blue perennial bed, it skirts the shade of the big walnut beside the secluded north windows of the house, and enters the shade of the horse chestnut. The chestnut, a venerable symbol whose bad garden habits are tolerated, interrupts the flow, but beyond it the grass sweeps on to the northern limit of the garden. On the west side, against Middle Turn's garden wall, which is draped in green and variegated *Hedera colchica*, is a border of greens and gold – variegated hollies, choisya, pyrancathas, ferns and woodruff. Here also, *Euphorbia robbiæ*, a pest to some gardeners, but liked here for the story that it came home from China in Mrs Robb's bonnet box.

Opposite the green and gold border, the lawn, which has flowed like a green river across the whole of the main garden, is brought to a definite stop in a straight line against a beech and yew hedge. A break in the hedge reveals that it is paralleled by a straight and narrow path of the deeply-etched stable floor blocks; they look rather like chunky chocolate blocks when wet. This chocolate block path, stopped at the garden end with a thatched dovecote (a memento from Rachel's childhood) in a curl of beech hedge, slips northwards into the little box court behind the coach house. Here it ends in a chocolate block circle, not quite complete, paired to the circle holding the dough mixing bowl, which ends the central vista through the coach house. These two vistas, projected from the box court, are the strongest linear statements

in the main garden; inevitably they prompt reminders of how the walls and beams in the house are allowed to materialise into differing roles.

The speciality within the box court, which draws the gaze from the colourful annual bedding, is the row of shuttlecock fern, *Matteuccia struthiopteris*, lined in front of a fan-trained morello cherry on the north facing wall. A winter flowering of *Cyclamen coum* has been patiently cultivated beneath the ferns.

It is worth stealing into the office garden court again, for the quiet pleasure of the shade and the splash of the water, the sun perhaps slanting onto the topmost branches of the magnolia; the return journey offers changing lights. From the deep shade of the stepped doorway, the box court is invariably hot, at least half of it bathed in strong sunlight. Beneath the coach house arch there is shade and a cool breeze; the arch is hung with tools with pride of place for an old band-saw which once worked in Walter Rose's carpenter's shop. The former stable, hay rack and trough complete, is an enviable earthy, dark, potting shed. Then, out into the sunlight again, into the daisy garden. And why the Daisy garden? This is the lowest point of the garden, with pitiably little soil over the limestone bedrock. In despair of growing anything Peter consulted John Brookes, whose immediate response was "daisies". It proved a brilliant inspiration, for the daisy form fits the octagonal paving of the space and, after breaking up some of the bedrock and building up the surrounding soil, asters and chrysanthemums and their kind have made a late summer flowering here. Whilst they are preparing themselves, pots of annuals and pelargoniums in rioting scarlets and reds are set out.

From the low viewpoint of the daisy garden, especially in the late afternoon sun, the tree peony, roses, grasses, bamboos and euphorbias

Self seeded *Cotoneaster horizontalis* against a stone trough.

around the pergola become a jungle of sunny fronds against the sky. It is a modest climb to the pergola, but enough for a sense of achievement. New choices await, right – through the flowers to the central sunny glade, the heart of the garden regained, – or left, down cleverly angled gravel and sleeper steps into the eastern glade. The steps are set with pots holding tender treasures, daturas and abutilons are favourites. In the eastern glade there is a small brick "sittery" against the wall of the office court, and this is the best place to remain unfound. When such delicious retreat has

to end, the low road, the grass sweep of the eastern glade, leads round into the sunny centre of things once more. There, as if on a stage, sits the urn, its rough surface dappled in sunlight, its solid, pure curve seen in greatest contrast to the delicate luminosity of its companion, a tall birch, with chalk-white peeling bark, *Betula platyphylla szechuanica*. But from this beautiful stranger, from half a world away, it is just a few steps along the randomly paved paths of the spring woodland, now heavy with summer green, to Turn End's garden door, and the heart of the house.

Far right:
The front door with its friendly lamp, and parcel sized letter-box below a broad shelf for shopping and milk bottles, invites the visitor and opens into an area barely 1.5 metres wide but the glass wall over the pond takes the eye on and out.

Right:
Turn left and the metre wide 'corridor' passing the dining table, is a vista through house and garden suggesting further spaces left and beyond.

Opposite:
The reverse view from the living room passes the front door and is terminated by the wichert wall of the studio (see page 18). The absence of doors and full height walls enables sunlight to flood throughout.

Below:
The apparent spaciousness of the kitchen beyond the dining table belies its tiny footprint.

Above:
The living room, with morning sun streaming through its high east window, is under 3 metres wide, but 9 metres long. This format provides a cosy fireside space at one end, and…

Right:
…extends at the other into a garden room for sleeping or additional seating. The floor reaches out without interruption into the courtyard.

Opposite:
The end wall is extended by light entering through a glazed roof against the wichert boundary wall. The gallery over has been both music room and store. Further storage is under built-in seating and bed.

The kitchen looks out over the courtyard and through a wichert arch into No-mans. Water iris and cotton grass grow on the edge of the pond. *Marrubium cylleneum* grows over a sunny rock in front of the arch. See page 8 for the reverse view.

Troughs of alpines and pans of sempervivum decorate the hot gravel area of No-mans with sun loving perennials beyond.

Above:
No-mans is bounded on its south side by this pergola which provides a visual stop while allowing sunlight to pass through. The path is made from railway sleepers. Roses in soft colours, honeysuckle, blackberries and *Actinidia chinensis* (Kiwi fruit) climb over the rough timber poles.
Right:
A medley of late summer flowers with eremurus seed heads.

No-mans is visually enclosed by the High Street houses to its east. The cottage garden character here avoids any temptation to dominate them. Flowering are: Iris 'Langport Star' and 'Langport Wren', *Asphodeline lutea* and *Eremurus himalaicus*.

No-mans looking south to the pergola in May. Gravel paths make a cruciform pattern between beds raised with railway sleepers. This strong geometric structure allows the planting to be exuberant without losing its form. (see plan page 38) Plants on the left of the path are in mainly warm, bright colours which relate to the terracotta tiles of the wichert walls, while those on the right are in softer shades.

Above:
Autumn in the woodland
garden with the high east
window framed by old apple
trees and more recently planted
birches. (see pages 14 and 62)

Opposite:
The closely mullioned window
dominates both the view
through the house and the
woodland garden (above). The
height of the timber shelf to
the left of the concrete block
pillar was determined by a wish
to allow sunlight to spill over
into the kitchen.

Opposite:
Looking from the chestnut tree along the curving grass glade between the spring garden and summer borders with Monica Young's urn acting as a focus and reference point back to the house. To the right, out of this picture is the central walnut tree and…
Left:
…Middle Turn's high east facing living room window looking into the walnut branches. Its timber mullions allow light to flood in yet maintain privacy. This shady corner grows ferns, lily of the valley, winter flowering cyclamen and various ivies.

Early morning sun lights Turn
End bedrooms and Middle
Turn living room beyond the
walnut tree. (see previous
page) Bedroom cills are nearly
at eye level from outside
providing more privacy than is
usual for a ground floor room.

The guest room at Turn End
looking out in the evening.
The raised floor and eye level
eaves beam make the window
friendly and private with an
extensive garden view.

A cast glass ceiling gives an intimate scale and scintillating feel to the small landing space, borrowing light from the south facing clerestory over the bathroom. The richness of form and colour and the height of this room belie its tiny floorspace, only the width of a bath.

The landing and bedrooms beyond, guest room on right. (see page 95)
The wall on the right screens the dressing room (a necessary adjunct to the living room's built-in bed); a concrete dressing table projects through. Bedroom doors are simple timber boards clamped between vertical battens, handles are also made of wood.

Timber details in the studio
Right:
The concrete block pillar
supports a beam and rafters
for the car-port roof behind
the wichert wall and
translucent glass window
which is lit at night. This
device enabled us to
incorporate the wichert wall
into the house without its
carrying a load. Detail is simple
and direct.
Opposite:
A removable ladder to a
sleeping gallery over the
studio, built when it was made
into a bedroom for Clair and
Rachel. The gallery is bolted to
hangers from the roof. Visual
richness is achieved with
simple junctions between
elements.
In details like these every
component used in the
building contributes to the
finished product, nothing is
hidden.

This page and opposite:
Opposing views of the same pillar. Every element has its purpose. Here the pillar supports the main beam over the dining area (see pages 83, 90) and heavy timbers forming bookshelves in the living room, as well as enclosing and growing horizontally to become the built-in seats. The pillar on the left of both pictures carries an eaves beam for the dining area and the main beam supporting the living room gallery. (see page 84)

Morning sunlight from the high east window penetrating through the living room and over the shelves into the kitchen.

Garden details and a delight in textures.
Above and left:
Morello cherry trained into a fan behind the shuttlecock fern, *Matteuccia struthiopteris*. In front are antirrhinums within a box hedge.
Opposite:
The urn surrounded by a flower spike and leaves of *Rheum palmatum*, contrasting with newly opened fern fronds and flowers of *Polygonum bistorta* 'Superbum' with a 'black' hellebore in the foreground.

The eastern glade, views looking both ways from the same spot.
Right:
The urn terminates this vista. Note the proximity of High Street houses behind the garden wall, emphasising our village centre location. *Rosa cantabrigiensis* dominates this area in May with New Zealand flax, *Phormium tenax* on the left.
Opposite:
The glade is terminated by the 'sittery', the most secret part of the garden and the best place in which to remain unfound! On the left is a tall bamboo, *Semiarundinaria fastuosa*. To the right of the brick enclosed sittery is a paper-bark birch, *Betula x fetisowii* with Spanish gorse, *Genista hispanica* in front.

We formed this arch in the back wall of the coach house to enable the vista from the square pergola, through the daisy garden, to terminate at the cast iron urn in the box hedged court. In a former incarnation the urn was a dough mixing bowl. Its shape, though extremely satisfying, was designed purely for that function, but it now forms the centrepiece to annual bedding schemes

Bedding schemes and colours vary from spring to summer and year to year.
Above:
Dwarf lobelia, one of the most successful as it eventually forms an almost perfect carpet.

Far left, top:
Yellow and white pansies in spring.
Far left, bottom:
Orange and yellow wallflowers. *Ceanothus* 'Cascade' on the south wall is not always a happy companion to the bedding colours!
Left:
Another summer scheme with pink impatiens and ruby nicotiana. The urn is planted with *Erysimum* 'Bowles' Mauve' and *Osteospermum ecklonis*

Photos this page, Peter Aldington

Opposite:
Morning sunlight reaches the daisy garden. This strongly centralised formal area provides a pause between the square pergola and the coach house. The profusion of planting is augmented in summer by pots. There is also a cross axis from a seat on the right through a gap in the hedge opposite to the area beneath the horse chestnut. (see plan page 71)

Left:
The Office garden ends the sequence of formal gardens. A glass door off right gives the office access to the circular pool. *Wisteria floribunda* 'Macrobotrys' in early May. The brick containers are filled with imported and lime free soil. This has enabled us to grow a camellia, a magnolia and various rhododendrons. (see opposite view page 72)

The Turn and Middle Turn at night. The houses accept admirable restraint or voluptuous furnishing equally well.
Right:
The dining area in The Turn seen from the living room three steps below. This is the point at which the site slope down from Townside is absorbed, making a positive attribute out of it rather than taking the 'easy' option of 'losing' it between houses.
Opposite:
The living room in Middle Turn, richly decorated, is identical in form to that at Turn End and makes an interesting contrast (see page 85). The hanging loft staircase was a later addition replacing a ladder.

The opposite end of Middle Turn living room from the previous page. A golden light enhances the warmth and comfort achieved by John and Betty.

The same view in Turn End's living room with only a central light. Notice how flat and uninteresting the space becomes! Contrast this with the next two pages.

In this picture taken from the identical position to the previous one, light is reflected off the paper globe instead of coming from it. The end wall and roof are lit with floods, and spot lights provide bright pools of light on seats and carpet. Most of us spend more time in our living rooms in winter using artificial light than we do in summer daylight, yet we rarely explore the creative possibilities of modern lighting technology.

Here the different colour of light on the globe has changed the atmosphere. The cushions have not changed but a light has been moved to enhance their colours. All the effects in these three scenes are achieved by pressing switches!

endwords

For over thirty years Turn End's structural integrity has been the constant background to changing possessions and patterns of life: it has proved to be flexible, and adaptable. With the arrival of Clair and Rachel it became a family home, as well as an architect's office. In 1979 when the office moved to no. 6 High Street, the girls took over the studio, with a sleeping balcony inserted, which occupies the secluded territory behind the swing of the front door at the west end of the house. Now that Clair and Rachel have homes of their own, Peter has retrieved the studio. Margaret has her desk in one of the quiet, north facing rooms, and the other is a guest bedroom. Some older visitors find the open plan disconcerting, particularly as the Aldingtons have their bed in the living room: others, sometimes younger, find the candour appealing, and appreciate the notion of snow swirling against the glass at the end of the bed, or – with the glazed doors open in summer – of sleeping beneath the stars.

Modern architecture was always intended to sweep away Victorian boxed-living and secrecy, and also to dispense with drudgery. Turn End has proved its credentials here too; the exterior roughcast has only needed painting twice in thirty years, the interior walls have been emulsioned in parts, as and when proved necessary, but with no great upheavals. Most of the interior wood has never needed re-varnishing, and it and the other wipe clean surfaces have wiped clean. The insulation has proved effective, and in the 1960s the cost of electric underfloor heating was estimated at £1 per week. On this point the architect has most regrets, for from that far-away perspective electricity was the fuel of the future, but now it is too expensive and today he would choose differently.

Two views of Turn End studio with morning sunlight from the east-facing window over the courtyard pool.
This room has had three incarnations: first as a practice office, then with the added sleeping gallery, our daughters' room; it now doubles as a study and television room. This ability to accept change is an answer by example to those who say the design lacks flexibility.

Turn End's first gardener, Mary de la Rue, started in August 1977. Mary came for a year, but stayed for what she regards as her seven-year apprenticeship with Peter, which enabled her to go on to work for the National Trust. She was followed briefly by Polly Avery, and then Dawn Meadows, the present gardener, came in 1987. Dawn's interest in gardening had led her to a "wider opportunities" course in Liverpool, where she finished up as an instructor. Rewarding as this was, she decided that she really wanted to live in the country, so she answered Peter's advertisement, and in her words, "we seemed to suit each other". Dawn does all the seed raising and propagating, she has taken the growing celebrity status of the garden in her quiet stride, and her devotion to her charge is palpable everywhere. The garden runs on a no-digging regime, with everything composted and everywhere mulched; chemicals are used when absolutely necessary.

The first opening for the National Gardens Scheme was with other Haddenham gardens in June 1981, the first independent opening was on 29 April 1984. Since then the garden has been open regularly for the Scheme and for other charities. It now entertains a growing number of private group visits from architects and gardeners, from here and abroad. Once a year, in summer, house and garden have been opened for design professionals,

students and interested "others". From the outset the village housing has attracted press coverage and magazine articles, particularly surrounding its RIBA Award in 1970, and the garden's maturity has inspired a repeat flush. A bibliography of the major articles is on page 123.

Turn End wears its fame lightly, and the Aldingtons have absorbed their rather larger than usual number of visitors into their busy lives. Now, however, their hearts are set on a more northerly horizon for at least part of the year; the future of Turn End will be in the hands of a charitable trust, of which more details are noted opposite.

The garden, 'still evolving, though not as hectically as it used to' is now more important than ever as a rich, green oasis in the centre of a much more intensively built-up Haddenham. The trees that they fought to keep are now elderly, others have already been lost, and the nurture of replacements is the important task. Much to Peter's disdain he finds he may one day have to re-plant his least favourite garden tree, for this whole story – as it turns out – spins on a horse chestnut bud. The future guardians of Turn End will need *Aesculus hippocastanum* on hand, to remind them of Le Corbusier's admiration of the exploding bud – 'a great lesson in exactitude of foresight, in eloquence of form, in fantasy through diversity'.[24]

Note:
24. Le Corbusier and Francois de Pierrefeu, *The Home of Man*, Architectural Press, 1948, p 133

Turn End Charitable Trust was formed on June 20, 1998. Its objects are, '*for the benefit of the public generally:*

'*1. The sympathetic conservation, protection and maintenance of the properties and the garden as evolving or living entities, as designed or laid out by Peter John Aldington and to make them available for the use and the benefit of the public;*

'*2. the advancement of education and scholarship in the art of building and garden design and in so doing to foster the integration of these two disciplines into a single indivisible process, each element to interact with and be dependent on the other;*

'*3. the promotion of public knowledge and understanding of architecture, planning, landscape architecture and allied subjects.*'

The Turn, Middle Turn, Turn End, and retaining walls were added to the list of buildings of special architectural or historic interest on July 15, 1998.

writer's acknowledgements

Note: All unpublished sources, except where noted otherwise, are in the Turn End archives.
All unattributed quotations are from Peter Aldington.

I would like to acknowledge the sources for my quotations and particularly my thanks to Lord Esher for permission to quote from his 1964 Report and his more recent letter to Peter Aldington. I am also very grateful for courteous assistance at Buckinghamshire County Archives, the County Reference Library and at Aylesbury Vale District Council Offices.

For illuminating and helpful conversations, my thanks to Diana Alderson, Reg, Win and Rex Carslake, Roger Smith, Colin Stillwell, John and Hazel Creaser, John and Betty Landon, Mary de la Rue and Dawn Meadows. My special appreciation to Rachel Aldington and Clair Aldington Jackson, because I have been writing about their home, and thanks to Darrell Jackson and Donald Wilson for their constructive criticism and support. Last, but hardly least, now that my effort is nearly over, I am rather overwhelmed that Peter and Margaret Aldington should have asked me to write about their building adventures, and their garden. They have delved into their pasts and memories, as well as into the parcels and boxes of the Turn End archive, with endless patience. I have had the pleasures of many visits to them, the garden and three houses, which I hope will continue for many years to come.

Jane Brown, Elton, 1998

bibliography
articles or references appear in the following

Books:
Decorative Art in Modern Interiors, *Moody 1969/70*
Nuove Ville (Italy), *Roberto Aloi 1970*
Houses for Today, *June Park 1971*
Eingange (Germany), *Ossenberg & Djordjevic 1973*
Wohnen unter schragem Dach (Germany), *Annemarie Mutsch-Engel 1975*
Az en Hazam (Hungary), *Calmeyer-Rojko 1975*
The Brighter Side of Concrete, *George Perkin 1979*
Classic Modern Houses in Europe, *Einzig 1981*
Modern British Architecture since 1945,
ed. P Murray & S Trombley 1984
Collins Book of British Gardens, *Plumtre 1985*
Garden Open Today, *Martyn and Alison Rix 1987*
English Private Gardens, *Johnson & Berry 1991*
Susan Hampshire My Secret Garden, *Berry 1993*

Periodicals:
Concrete Quarterly, *July-Sept 1968; Jan-March 1983; Jan-March 1984; Jan-March 1985*
Architectural Review, *August 1968*
Deutsche Bauzeitung, *March 1969*
Progressive Architecture (USA), *June 1969*
Die Kunst und das' schone Heim (Germany) *March 1970*
RIBA Journal, *July 1970; February 1979*
Architects Journal, *2.9.70; 8.8.84*
Homes & Gardens, *September 1970*
Bulletin, *October 1970*
Le Journal de la Maison (France), *October 1970*
Architecture & Urbanism (Japan), *February 1971*
Interni (Italy), *March 1971*
Outlook, *Summer 1971*
Ville Giardini (Italy), *July 1971*
Housing, Landscape & Concrete, *March 1976*
Building Design, *9.11.76*
Informes de la Construccion (Spain), *Jan/Feb.1977*
RIBA Journal, *February 1979*
Building Design, *7.9.79*
Popular Gardening, *22 October 1981*
Toshi-Jutaku (Japan), *July 1983*
Elementer Calendar *1985*
Country Life, *15 August 1985*
The Garden, RHS Journal, (article by P.A.) *July 1986*
Successful Gardening, (part work) *1988*
Architectural Review, *September 1989*
Practical Gardening, *May 1990*

Homes and Gardens, *June 1994*
Garden Design Journal, (article by P.A.) *Winter/Spring 1995/6*
Country Homes and Interiors, *April 1996*
Hampshire Gardens Trust Journal, *August 1996*
Perspectives, *Oct/Nov 1996*
RIBA Journal, *October 1996*
Femina (Sweden), *April 1997*
Good Housekeeping, *May 1997*
Home Ideas (Japan), *February 1997*
Harpers & Queen, *May 1998*

Newspapers:
The Times, *11.5.67; 1.7.70*
Observer Magazine, *May 1968*
Daily Telegraph, *9.9.68; 22.11.68*
Daily Mirror, *1.7.70*
Bucks Herald, *2.7.70; 22.10.70; 22.8.95; 14.7.98*
Bucks Advertiser, *2.7.70*
Thame Gazette, *7.7.70; 27.10.70*
Daily Mail, *8.9.70*
Oxford Times, *3.7.70; 16.10.70; 23.10.70*
Oxford Mail, *21.5.74; 24.3.98*
The Times Saturday Review, *30 March 1991*
Bucks Herald Supplement, *Spring 1992*
Observer Life Magazine, *3 November 1996*
The Times Weekend, *24 January 1998*

Urn by Svend Bayer

photographer's comments

The working title adopted for this project by my office was 'Turn Never Ending' because of the seemingly continuous supply of transparencies that had to be checked and filed. This embodied a certain truth as there is no specific point in a project like this when one can say the job is done.

The exercises of communicating photographically the experiences and qualities of a garden as opposed to a building are similar but surprisingly different. Both involve space, light, colour and texture; however, in the case of the garden the fourth dimension soon becomes apparent, as the nature of space is ephemeral and indistinct. The characteristics differ each season, in fact changes occur on an almost daily basis. On a merely practical level, this led to my rarely being available at exactly the desired time.

Architecture is a static shell in which a multitude of differing activities can take place, whereas a garden is an ever changing organic entity. This project more than any other gave me the opportunity to make a direct comparison between photographing the buildings, where I was always looking for the perfect directional light to throw the characteristics into sharp relief, and the garden where I soon learnt that flat lighting often produced the favoured results.

The terms beauty, harmony and delight seem to hark back to a pre-renaissance era of architectural philosophy, but no expressions are more relevant to photographing this project. Sadly, because of the subtleties and complexities involved, pictures can only hint at the experience, but it was fascinating to try.

Richard Bryant, Kingston on Thames 1998

product and material suppliers:

Foamed concrete blocks, *Durox Building Products*
Timber: (Turn End), *Dolton Bournes & Dolton Ltd*
(The Turn, Middle Turn), *R.J. Johnson, Oxford*
Aluminium nails, *J. Stone and Company Ltd*
Delta concrete roof tiles, *Redland Tiles Ltd*
Roof flashings, *'Faroled', Farmiloe Sealants Ltd*
Insulation, *'Marleycel', The Marley Tile Co Ltd*
Quarry tiles (12ins square), *Stanley Bros Ltd*
Double glazing units, *Plyglass Ltd*
Other glazing, *James Clark & Eaton Ltd*
Louvre windows, *'Naco', N.V. Appleton Ltd*
Sliding folding door gear, *P.C. Henderson Ltd*
Draught excluders, *'Kez Strip', Kleen-e-ze Brush Co*
Door & window seals, *Herts Rubber Company*
Sliding door gear, *E. Hillaldam & Co Ltd*
Door & window furniture:
(Turn End), *Dryad Metal Works Ltd,*
(The Turn, Middle Turn), *G.& S. Allgood Ltd*
Espagnolette bolts, *'Bico', H.& C. Davis & Co Ltd*
Curtain tracks, *'Rolls Miniglide', W.A. Hudson Ltd*
Polyurethane varnish, *'Abercorn', Pinchin Johnson*
Paint, *'Exelflat' emulsion, Cementone Ltd*
Plumbing & drainage parts, *Kay and Co Ltd*
Sanitary ware, *'Lotus', Adamsez Ltd*
Baths, *'Swallow', Carron*
Taps, *Barking Brassware Ltd*
Shower valve, *'Temperfix', F.H. Bourner & Co*
Stainless steel sinks, *W.& G. Sissons Ltd*
Oven & hotplates, *'Credaplan', Simplex Electric Co*
Stainless hotplate surround, *Elliotts of Reading*
Refrigerator, *'Hotpoint Iced Diamond', A.E.I. Ltd*
Floor heating cables, *'Aerialite'*
Heating control, *'Miniprobe', Findlay, Irvine Ltd*
Fan assisted storage heaters, *Revo Electric Co*
Light fittings, *Rotaflex (G.B.) Ltd*
Outside lights glassware, *Laboratory Glassblowers*
Boot scraper, *G.A. Harvey Group Services Ltd*
Entrance mat, *'Nuway'*
House name signs, *Bribond Signs*
General building supplies, *Blanchford & Co Ltd,*
Dolton Bournes and Dolton Ltd
Rocks, Turn End courtyard, *Witney Stone Co Ltd*
Peat & peat blocks, *The Eclipse Peat Co Ltd*
Trees & shrubs, *Hilliers, Jackmans of Woking*
Shrub roses, *Sunningdale Nurseries*
Herbaceous perennials, *Bressingham Gardens*
Alpines, *Joe Elliott, W.E.Th. Ingwersen Ltd*

specialist trades and craftsmen:

Site clearance, *J Springell, Tom Nimmo*
Blockwork (Turn End) *Reg Saunders*
Blockwork (Turn, Middle Turn), *David Hawkes*
Roof construction *Peter Aldington*
Woodwork (Turn End) *Peter Aldington*
Glazed doors & special joinery, *Ivor Newton & Son*
Woodwork (Turn, Middle Turn), *Laishley & Cozens*
Other joinery, *Gordon Phipps*
Electrical equipment & installation, *George Williams*
Floor tiling, *A.W.H. Saville*
Steel chimneys, *Robert G. Green*
Outside lights metalwork, *Robert G. Green*
Roof tiling (Turn,Middle Turn), *Roy Pearce*
Sanding all woodwork & decorating, *Colin Stillwell,*
Roger Smith, Chris Vincent
Large stoneware urn, *Monica Young*
Other garden stoneware ornaments, *Svend Bayer*

index of plants

There are many hundreds of plants, shrubs and trees in the garden at Turn End. The following appear in the text (light numbers) or in captions (bold numbers)

Acæna buchananii

general index
text entries light numbers, captions bold, footnotes italic

This barrel slowly collapsed during the period of Richard Bryant's visits, and he called it 'self-destructing art'.